WHAT PEOPLE ARE SAYING ABOUT

Australian Druidry

Julie Brett's introduction to Australian Druidry is filled with information and inspiration for anyone who wants to connect with the sacred landscape of Australia. Drawing on her years of practical study into the plants, animals and seasons of the Great Southern Land, she outlines the nature festivals she has identified and the rituals she performs, while also teaching readers how to create their own connection and their own ceremonies based on their unique location.

Julie's form of Druidry is one of gratitude, contemplation and deep intuition and connection, and she shares her wisdom and experiences not to tell others how they should practice, but to encourage them to weave their own personal spiritual path. It includes many great references too, but also inspires you to find your own meanings and connect to nature in your own way. A wonderful resource for all Australians, and anyone interested in southern hemisphere magic...
Serene Conneeley, author of the *Sacred Sites* series of books

It's a fantastic piece of work and I think of interest to Druids beyond Australia's shores, this is a map for creating Druidry that is rooted in your own particular soil, wherever that soil is.
Nimue Brown, author of *Druidry and the Ancestors*

Julie Brett's *Australian Druidry* is a wonderfully practical and thoughtful approach to Australian Druidry. I love reading Julie Brett's work. It draws me into new ways of understanding and practicing my relationship with the other-than-human world. This book is the most recent in a long tradition of excellent books by Australian Pagans that creatively explore the Wheel of the

Year and other aspects of being Pagan in the Southern Hemisphere. Each one has taken Australian Pagans a step further along the road, and Julie Brett's book is an important contribution to that journey.

Douglas Ezzy, author of *Practising the Witch's Craft* and *Sex, Death and Witchcraft.*

This is a clearly written and creative guide to the practice of Druidry in the southern hemisphere. For those wakeful to their European ancestry or inspired to explore its teachings, the book encourages a sensitive relationship with the antipodean landscape, its climate and ecology, celebrating its uniqueness, while not intruding upon the native traditions.

Emma Restall-Orr, author of *Spirits of the Sacred Grove*

Pagan Portals
Australian Druidry

Connecting with the Sacred Landscape

Pagan Portals
Australian Druidry

Connecting with the Sacred Landscape

Julie Brett

MOON
BOOKS

Winchester, UK
Washington, USA

First published by Moon Books, 2017
Moon Books is an imprint of John Hunt Publishing Ltd., Laurel House, Station Approach,
Alresford, Hants, SO24 9JH, UK
office1@jhpbooks.net
www.johnhuntpublishing.com
www.moon-books.net

For distributor details and how to order please visit the 'Ordering' section on our website.

Text copyright: Julie Brett 2016

ISBN: 978 1 78535 370 3
978 1 78535 371 0 (ebook)
Library of Congress Control Number: 2016951868

A CIP catalogue record for this book is available from the British Library.

Design: Stuart Davies

Printed and bound by CPI Group (UK) Ltd, Croydon, CR0 4YY, UK

We operate a distinctive and ethical publishing philosophy in all
areas of our business, from our global network of authors to
production and worldwide distribution.

CONTENTS

Prologue and Thanks

Thank you to all the people who helped me with the writing of this book, from the very beginning of the circles I ran, to the Druids Down Under online community and all our lengthy discussions over the years, to those who helped me with research and forming the written material. Special thanks go my mentor Morgan Rhys Adams who introduced me to Druidry. Also to Tom Byrom, with whom I have had many a ritual, adventure in the bush, and long conversations on the book's topics. Particularly I'd like to thank you on your insights into the three ancestors. I'd like to thank Emma Restall-Orr for your incredible writing that has inspired me so much, and for your encouragement and insightful advice on editing. Thank you to Douglas Ezzy for expanding my mind through studying with you and Neville Drury for that summer course at the University of Tasmania, and also for your encouragement and help with editing. Thanks to Katrena Friel for your enthusiasm and helping it all come together clearly, as well as giving me the push to believe I could really do this. Thank you to Adrienne Piggott for allowing me to include your beautiful song lyrics and to Philip Shallcrass for your version of The Song of Amergín. A sincere thank you also everyone who has attended my Druids Down Under circles, and to the many people in the Pagan community in Sydney and other parts of Australia for your support and encouragement.

I'd like to thank my parents for giving me such an appreciation for nature, and for bringing us here to Australia from the UK with wide eyes and wonder at the beauty of this very different landscape. Thanks for all the bushwalks, camping trips and long talks about life, the universe and everything. Thank you also for encouraging me to study and to follow what I am passionate about. You've shaped me more than you know.

And finally I would like to thank my husband for his patience.

I have been working on this book the whole time I've known you! Thank you for all your support and encouragement. And thanks to my son Lugh who was a tree hugger before he could talk. Your natural love of the bush gives me so much hope for the future of our world.

In the peace of the grove
Julie Brett
/ | \

Part 1: Introduction

Australia has a diverse landscape, unique plants and animals, and seasons that incorporate fire and flood, drought and also times of great abundance. The mood of the landscape can change from one valley to the next, and differs greatly from the north to the south, and from the coast to the red centre, yet every part of it has something to tell us. Australian Druidry is a spiritual path of connecting with the Australian landscape as a sacred place. It is a method of listening to the messages the land has for us, and coming into communication with its unique voice. Modern Druidry is a path of nature-based spirituality being walked by many people over the world today. It centers on an understanding that it is the 'wisdom of the trees' as the messages of the natural world that can help us find guidance in our lives for peace, learning, and personal development. These meanings can help guide our lives and bring us into connection with the spirit that flows through all things. Moving into alignment with the natural world can inspire us and guide us towards greater creativity and happiness in life.

In our connection with nature we feel the presence of the divine; in the turn of the seasons we feel changes in our own being; in our encounters with animals we see messages for our lives; in the presence of trees we feel their wisdom. For those who learn to listen, the land itself speaks. In Australian Druidry we explore and develop new traditions through these interactions in the native landscape, as well as drawing on a wealth of historical spiritual traditions of those practicing in other lands. Modern Druidry in any landscape is a process of finding a personal connection with nature and spirit, and is a tradition that is evolving and changing as we explore. As John Michael Greer puts it:

Modern Druids learn from ancient teachings, the developing tradition of modern Druidry itself and the every-changing lessons of the living Earth. They embrace an experiential spirituality and forsake rigid belief systems for disciplines of inner development and personal contact with the realms of nature and spirit.

Modern Druidry is part of a larger phenomenon of neo-Pagan (or simply 'Pagan') traditions, which are nature-based spiritualities that look to pre-Christian mythology and folklore for inspiration and guidance, but are also highly explorative, experimental and developing form. These modern spiritual paths are often more personalized, flexible, intuitive in regards to practices, and have little structure or centralized authority in terms of organization or hierarchical systems. Rather they find their authority in nature, and an expectation of personal experience of the spiritual. As Graham Harvey has explained, 'For those who name themselves Pagan it means 'those who honor the Earth'.' So, in this sense, our only authority is our relationship with the Earth and with nature. That relationship is our guiding principle.

Though there is often a great deal of reverence and respect given to traditions of the past, this sense of honoring the Earth gives a lot of room for new ideas to form and for exploration into new ways of practicing a spirituality, particularly in areas of the world not formerly connected within those historic traditions. Our practice then becomes simultaneously based on the old ways, and at the same time is a process of exploration in a different and new landscape for that tradition. It is a process of exploring directly as well as respectfully interacting with Indigenous cultures that have already been listening here for a long time.

The seasons, animals and plants in Australia have a unique story to tell. Their messages are in no way less than those of any other land. The symbols of Kangaroo, Dingo or Kookaburra are just as powerful as those of Lion, Wolf or Eagle. The wattle and eucalyptus trees are just as important as the oak and the holly. The seasons here are not 'weird' or 'wrong' because they don't follow the systems laid out for the cycles of other places; they are just different, unique and special in their own way. There is a great wealth of knowledge available to us in the symbols of this sacred landscape. Connecting with its spirit, and the wisdom in Druidry, helps us find our wholeness and a true sense of belonging in this land.

In this book you'll find practical information on understanding the energies, meanings and symbols of the seasons in the place you live. It will help you, no matter where you live, to gain the tools and methods needed to understand the symbols of the seasons, plants, animals and spirits, and create meaningful rituals to celebrate them. The section on the Three Ancestors will help you see how this practice is relevant to people of many different backgrounds and beliefs. You can take from this book what is relevant to you, and let the rest be. I have presented this information as a part of Druidry because that's how I found it, but the word 'Druid' is thought to mean 'the wisdom of the trees', which means it is a path relevant to all of us interested in the wisdom of nature.

The people of Australia are as diverse as the landscape. We come from many different backgrounds and have many different personal influences and interests. Recognizing this is relevant to modern Druidry. As well as being a nature-based spirituality, it is a spirituality of recognition of our ancestors. The ancestors are all the people who have come before us whether in our family or the lines of teachings we have received in our lives, or those who came before us in the land we live in. Without these people we would not be who we are today. Learning to adapt our practice to our local area and also to the diversity of the people we practice with, are two of the main goals of this book.

You will come to see a way of interacting with the Australian landscape as a sacred place, full of wisdom and spiritual guidance, that we are an important part of as keepers and guardians. You will find a way informed by the wisdom of the ancient Druids and modern Druidry alike, which deeply respect the ancestors of the land and the spirits that dwell within it and in each of us. I hope this book helps you to connect with this very special sacred landscape and continue the evolving journey of Australian Druidry.

Defining Australian Druidry

Australian Druidry could be defined as the practice of 'Druidry' or 'modern Druidry' in a way that is applicable to the Australian landscape and its inhabitants, but I think it is more than that. It's an invitation to explore and to create. Modern Druidry is a path in which we must discern from our historical inspirations and the legend of the ancient Druids what is relevant to us today, and what is not. The groundwork has already been laid over the past few decades. Bringing these ideas to an Australian context is just another step in this expansion of ideas and the process of making them relevant to our lives today.

Druidry is a living tradition in which new ideas can flourish. Our study of the ancient Druids encourages us to learn about natural philosophy, honoring our ancestors and expressing our inspiration through our arts and poetry. In these ways Druidry provides an excellent path for the exploration of the Australian landscape. It provides a means for us to understand the Australian seasons, plants and animals; to understanding our identity through our diverse ancestry; and to become inspired by the spirit of the land here and to express our connection with it. Australian Druidry then can be defined as the practice of Druidry as a process of discerning ancient Druidic wisdom's relevance to our lives today, and bringing that into the Australian context.

The ancient Druids existed among the Celtic and Gaulic people of Europe. According to the Romans and Greeks they were natural philosophers, moral philosophers and advisers to kings. In addition to those called Druids, there were also poets called Bards, and Ovates who worked with the spirit world for divination and magic. Modern Druidry is inspired by what little we know of the ancient Bards, Ovates and Druids, but there is no direct lineage of teaching reaching into the past. The wisdom of the Druids in their own time was a strictly oral tradition and so there are no written records that we can reliably draw on. We can, however, find remnants of their teaching in folklore and mythology, place names, archaeology, some of the surviving traditions of the Bards, which lasted into the 17th century, and other sources. There are also the practices of the 'fraternal Druids' or revivalist Druids of the 18th century friendly societies. Some of these practices and ideas, such as the imaginings of Iolo Morganwg, have also been important to the exploration and reimagining of modern Druidry.

Much in Druidry has had to be rediscovered, patched back together, intuited and creatively developed over the past few decades. As Professor Ronald Hutton argues, 'We can know virtually nothing of certainty about the ancient Druids so that – although they certainly existed – they function more or less as legendary figures.' I would argue that the legend of the Druids inspires modern Druidry more than anything.

The legend of the Druids has been imagined and shaped to modern purposes and personal biases in many different ways over the years since their disappearance. Professor Ronald Hutton describes these different forms of the Druids as: the Patriotic Druids, the Wise Druids, the Green Druids, the Demonic Druids, the Fraternal Druids, and the Rebel Druids, also pondering the potential for the Future Druids. My own legend of the Druids is a blend of the Wise, Green and Rebel Druids, all with a very optimistic spin. Our legends are powerful because they represent what we would have for ourselves. Our heroes always represent our best selves. I envision the Druids as 'Wise' because I imagine they meditated long and hard about how to live a good life and what it is to be a good person; I see them as 'Green' because I would hope that they cared for the Earth and were in connection with nature, speaking with the trees and animals, reflecting on the seasons, and understanding omens; and 'Rebels' because they would have been open, experimental and would base their sense of truth on personal connection with nature rather than centralized authority.

I am aware that this is dreaming; that it is a fanciful spin on the legend, not based on an empirically provable reality, but more about what I *want* to believe. Even so, I think that dreams are the place from where mythology springs. For me, Druidry is a spiritual path that holds the mythology of the Druids as legends and heroes at its heart. The Druids to me are the wizards and wild women who know the song of the land and live in harmony with it, both then and now. The land guides their lives and brings them inspiration and peace, and it's this optimistic vision of the Druids that I shamelessly seek out in the myths and other information I can find about the Druids. I am very interested in historical accuracy, but I don't find it integral to what inspires me. Rather than seeking to recreate a practice in perfect alignment with the historical Druids, I am much more concerned with what's relevant to my life and the world I live in. One based on personal connection with nature that feels good and right, helps me to be a better person and to feel whole, creative and happy. I find all these things in Druidry. Rather than trying to emulate the past, we imagine what the Druids of today might look like instead.

Pondering the idea of Australian Druidry in this regard, I believe we also need to reimagine a new legendary image of the Druid in Australia. If we can reimagine the Druid in the modern day, we can also come to imagine the Druid in the Australian landscape. Personally, I see those same wise woman and wizard-like characters I associate with the Druids, but now they are finding the wisdom of the Australian environment. They stand on the beach with the wallabies; they sit in the cave in the bush; they know the medicines, both physical and spiritual, of all the plants and animals; they encounter the sacred spaces and the energy of the ancestors here; they are wise, green and rebellious and very much in the here and now.

It is important to be aware in this that there are many modern forms of Druidry and the degree to which the people following these see themselves as experimental as opposed to reconstructing a historical tradition will certainly vary. I'm not claiming any authority, or definitive description of what 'Druidry' is. I am simply presenting you with my own experience. I hope it serves you in some way. Nevertheless, there is an element of exploration in every kind of modern Druidry that requires us to have discernment for what works for us, and you too will no doubt work out what is right for you. No matter what your personal stance is, the diversity and explorative nature of modern Druidry opens the way for us in understanding the Australian landscape, and our place within it. There is scope for us to make our own way and go with what feels right for us, finding our anchor in the wisdom of nature. It is my belief that for a spiritual path to 'work', it does not need to have a long history. It need only be relevant to our lives and help us find the sacred so that we can feel more at peace with our existence. In Australian Druidry our work is in how we interpret the wisdom of the ancient Druids, as well as the newer forms of modern Druidry, and have them make sense in our very different landscape.

So Australian Druidry is not just practicing Druidry in Australia, it is also an invitation to explore and create new practices, ideas and traditions, drawing on what already exists, and making it relevant. I believe being an Australian Druid today means adapting the practice of modern Druidry to our particular context of landscape, history, and ancestors, and finding ways to be inspired by these in our expression of our art, whatever form that might take.

We begin with exploring natural energies and symbols. One possible translation of the word 'Druid' is 'wisdom of the trees' with 'dru' meaning oak, or wood/tree, and 'uid' having the same root as 'wisdom' or 'wit'. This sentiment encourages us to look to the natural world for sources of wisdom. Unfortunately, the ancient Druids left no myths about gum trees that can help us to grasp their sacred meaning, so in our hopes to understand the sacredness of this land we need to delve into our study by other means. We might turn to Indigenous knowledge, and much can be learned there. However, it is important that we are also deeply aware of the need to respect and honor those traditions and not 'take' or appropriate their ideas. We are inspired by them, feel deep gratitude at being able to hear them, and find great wisdom in them, but also recognize the need to make our own inquiries into the sacredness of nature first hand. The wisdom of the trees can guide us directly, on a personal level.

Australian Druidry is a very practical path with much time dedicated to being in the bush, learning about the nature of the seasons, animals and plants, and their messages for us. Unfortunately, many of us have been brought up in a culture that often seems to fight against what is happening in nature, in favor of the seasonal changes of distant lands. The popular celebrations of Christmas, Easter and Halloween all have seasonal symbols whose inappropriate timing in respect to what is going on around us are not lost on even the most spiritually uninterested people. In the middle of summer it is just plain weird to have fake snow, snowmen, reindeer and holly decorating our homes, let alone feeling obliged to eat a hot roast dinner and drink egg nog on a scorching summer's day. Easter eggs and springtime flowers might mark the new life of Jesus in Christian celebrations, but their Pagan origins were a symbol of the springtime in which this festival was chosen to be celebrated. In fact the word 'Easter' comes from the name Eostara, which is the name of an Anglo Saxon Goddess of the spring, and her festival had the same name. Easter was a celebration of springtime and a dying and resur-recting 'Sun God' before it ever had a Christian story of a dying and resurrecting 'Son of God'. However, here in Australia, it is celebrated in the autumn with the same decorations as it is in the rest of the world.

As we learn about our land's energy, symbols and messages, and recognize the lines of ancestors who have influenced our being in this moment, we begin to learn about the flow of Awen. Awen comes from Welsh and means 'flowing spirit'. It is this flowing spirit that we feel inspires us to create our art. This might be in the form of poetry, songs, stories or other arts, which will in turn help others to feel that inspiration.

Quite a few authors have come before me on this creative journey and the explorative nature of other neo-Pagan traditions in Australia have a lot to share with Druidry. Particularly those who practice modern Witchcraft and Wicca, which share similarities with Druidry in their seasonal celebrations, inspirational mythologies of the past and experimental practice with a focus on the authority of connection with spirit and nature. You can find more information about these authors in the recommended reading section at the back of this book.

My Story

My coming to write on this subject has been a life-long journey for me. It is a subject dear to my heart. As a child I often found the popular celebrations of Christmas, Easter and Halloween, with their quite obviously inappropriate seasonal decorations, jarred with my sensibilities. Why did we have snowflakes decorating our home in the middle of summer? Why were we celebrating new life with eggs and spring flowers in the autumn, and what did it mean to dress up at Halloween as skeletons and ghosts? Questions like these led me to Paganism in my teenage years. I found the aspects of the celebrations that honored nature incredibly appealing. 'Finally,' I thought, 'a celebration of Yule in the winter time, and Eostara moved to the spring.' It sounded much more in line with the actual seasonal changes, but as I practiced these celebrations over the years I began to feel disconnected again. These celebrations, though seasonally adjusted by six months to fit our seasonal timing, still didn't speak of the magic of the bushland. I wanted to know why it was that those celebrations held the symbolism of specific plants, animals, colors and more.

So, in my twenties I spent 10 months living in the United Kingdom, with the goal of seeing a year through in its natural land, so that I could better understand the energy of Australia. I decided to try living in the beautiful town of Glastonbury, which I'd heard so much about through friends with spiritual interests. It was there that I first encountered the Druids. Having trouble finding a place to live, I was at the Isle of Avalon campsite for a few weeks in the summer. During that time the OBOD Summer Gathering was held and many attendees were camping in the field with us, though I didn't know anything about it at the time. One morning I woke up to the sound of 'Awen' being chanted right outside my tent. I can't say I was too happy about it at the time as I'd only managed to find a night shift job and had only gone to sleep a couple of hours before sunrise, but it was certainly an interesting introduction. Thinking of it these days I sometimes wonder if it was a blessing for my journey I never understood I was receiving until later! That was my first experience of Druids, though at that point it would still be a few weeks until I found out more about it.

I eventually got a job running a juice bar and cafe on the high street as a part of The Crown Hotel, and lived there in a room in the attic. While living there I attended a local Pagan pub meet up and met Morgan Rhys Adams, a Druid priestess who ran the circle at Avebury called The Gorsedd of Caer Abiri. We spoke about what I wanted to do and I explained I was looking for someone to teach me more about the local seasons and symbols. She offered to be my mentor and over the next few months taught me about Druidry while drinking tea at her home and spending time in the local forest areas. We also visited ancient burial tombs and old oak groves and spent time meditating there and discussing the path. I attended the circles she held at Avebury, and was initiated both there and at Stonehenge at the winter solstice into my Bardic grade in 2007. I should note, in Druidry, an 'initiation' is a beginning. To 'initiate' is to 'ignite' the fire in the head, which is Awen. It marks the beginning of our training, not the culmination of it, as it might refer to in other paths.

In our wanderings, circles and afternoons chatting I came to understand the relevance of the seasonal symbols, and what it was about them that made them sacred to their festivals. A particular plant would be unmissable in its relevance, the story of the season would be experienced by everyone, the activities of the festivals were those one would naturally be drawn to. It all started to make sense.

A significant moment came around midwinter. I was walking through a deciduous forest, the ground was covered with fallen leaves and the branches of all the trees were bare. In the distance

I saw a single holly tree, bright green and shining in the dim winter light. Its green color seemed magical in contrast to the dormant branches that surrounded it, and with that I knew I understood why it was such an important symbol of the season, and what I needed to do to begin my work back home. I had to look for signs like this one.

On my return I started taking notes on the seasonal changes, trawling my memory for patterns in years past. Looking for those holly tree moments and what it was that made the season special. I noticed changes in the moods of the seasons and kept a nature diary through the year. I also started holding open circles, not because I felt I was a leader, and certainly not an expert, but because I wanted to find like-minded people who would be interested in sharing this journey, and experimenting with how to celebrate the energy of the Australian seasons. I still consider myself no expert. I am just sharing with you what I have learned, in the hopes that we can learn more together. While in the UK I had started up a Facebook group called Druids Down Under to talk to people about what it means to follow the Druid path in the Australian landscape. This group led to the open circles that started soon after I returned and through them I was able to share my ideas, experiment with different ideas for ritual, hear the insights of others, and create a community of people who were similarly dedicated to connecting with this sacred landscape. My own observations and the insights that came to us as a group in the open circles and workshops have come together to create this book. I hope that by sharing it you will be more able to find your own way of connecting with the sacred landscape of your own area.

Now, let me tell you a story....

Journey to the Cave

The woman walked up the path in the heat of the summer's day. Sweat dripped down her back and she could feel it gathering at the base of her backpack. *The cicadas' song rang out clear and strong, pulsing in her mind as though in tune with her pounding heart – it had been a long climb. Wiping her brow and noticing the heat of her cheeks, she stepped up onto a rock platform and turned out to face the view. Out before her stretched a valley of green, a bit hazy as the eucalyptus oils in the air turned the distant hills a shade of blue. A flock of sulphur crested cockatoos rose from the trees with a cacophony of squawks, their white feathers bright against the dark blue of the high point of the sky. Seeing them, she knew her intuition was right. It was the right time. After savoring a taste of water from her bottle and noticing her mouth come alive with its touch, she turned from the view and continued on the path. The cave was just a little further along and it would be cooler there by the creek.*

She continued along the path that wound its way along and up the side of the hill through sandstone boulders and tall gums turned red from shedding their bark. A thicket of ferns and vines covered the ground and, in between, piles of fresh bark and leaves. Small lizards scampered away from her now and then as she made her way along the dirt track laced with gnarled roots and stepped sandstone slabs. Flies buzzed at her face, seeking out any moisture from eyes, nose or mouth. She waved a hand to shoo them as she walked, falling into a rhythm of the summer. This evening she would celebrate the Fire Festival and the blessings of the heat of summer, the lightest day, the shortest night. Though these hot days would continue for a good while to come, the light of the sun that fuelled their heat would be beginning to wane. Now was the time to feel the fiery energy around her and allow it to penetrate her consciousness, helping her to let go of what was no longer needed, to have gratitude for all she had achieved in the previous cycle, and to move into the next cycle. At this stage, she wasn't sure what that would be, she only knew she was ready.

She reached to her neck and touched her amulet: her fire amulet, red and brilliant, feeling warm from absorbing her body's heat and the heat of the day. It would help her to move into the fire energy tonight. Touching it she remembered the first Fire Festival where she had received it and charged it. That year the storms had come early and they celebrated both the energy of fire and storm as one. The day had been hot and in the afternoon the wind blew from the south and the kookaburras laughed at the bank of looming black clouds as they moved swiftly towards them up the coastline. Standing in the dry grass on the bank of the lagoon with her circle of friends, they had danced up the fiery crackling energy of the season, like a lightning bolt forming in the clouds. With drums and voices calling out, invoking the season's energy, 'I am the heat of the summer! I am the great southerly change! I am the lightning and the thunder! I am the dry grass beneath our feet, waiting for the rain!' The clouds had rumbled and flashed, echoing their energy, and soon the clouds came over them and it began to rain – hard, fat drops. They had danced the joy of the moment and the passing into the new phase; the heat and energy of the fires of the sun coming to meet the sacredness of water and rain. Intensity, release, refreshing, and rebirthing... She knew the Fire Festival would bring that energy again.

Looking up, she saw the rise of an outcrop of sandstone boulders and, below it, the darkness of the large hollow that would be her ritual space for the night. Nearby the creek babbled and flowed away down into the valley below, dripping over ledges and gushing and gurgling through holes. Beside the cave it opened out into a small pool. She put her bag down in the cave and took a long drink from her bottle of water. She could relax now, seeing the creek in good flow. At this time of year there was a good chance it would have dried out and every drop from her water bottle would have been precious nectar. But a few days of rain in the week prior had allowed for this journey, and for the ritual too. Though the day was hot and the fire energy high, the fire department's official ban on open fires was not in place today, and she could have a small fire for her ritual.

She looked at the cave around her. Like a gaping mouth or the cupped hands of the hill, it was a perfect place to stay. In the winter she had come here too. The fire that night had warmed the whole space and it felt cozy and comfortable, despite the chill on the air outside. She looked up to see the blackened roof and wondered how many people had called this cave home for the night over the years. She had heard that Indigenous people had used it too. She expected they would have used it when visiting the sacred site at the top of the hill where there were many carvings. She could almost feel them there still, like echoes on the wind. It felt homely and welcoming and she let out a sigh at finally having arrived.

Today in the cave it felt at least a couple of degrees cooler than any other place she had stopped, but she was still hot and sweaty from the hike up the hill. She left her things in the cave, took off her shoes and socks, and picked her way down the path towards the pool in the creek. Time to cleanse and prepare. She found a place on the rock where she could put her feet into the water, and reached her hand down to splash her face a little. The sensation was magical. She pulled off her clothing and moved back into the water, sinking down into the sandy bottom, all the while keeping an eye out for yabbies creeping around the rock edges.

The water was perfectly refreshing. Blissfully cool. She fully immersed herself and noticed the drone of the cicadas quieten to a distant whirr. As she resurfaced it was as though she was hearing them again for the first time. New life. Opportunity. Transformation. Taking a breath she rubbed at her body to clean off the grime of the journey, and had a final dip into the water, leaving her feeling cleansed and more connected with the space.

She left the water and found a rock to sit on in the shade. The warm air had her dry by the time she was ready to head back to the cave. Brushing back her hair, she noticed a kookaburra sitting in a branch across the water. His eye settled on her and he was still. 'Hello,' she said, happy to see her spirit animal. He ruffled his feathers and resettled them, and they looked at each other for a moment before he flew away towards the trees above the cave. 'Right o, it's about time to get ready I suppose,' she said and, after putting her clothes back on, moved back towards the cave.

The air had cooled a little and the light fading as the sun slowly made its way down. The cicadas eased their singing and made way for the kookaburra and his friends to call in the twilight. In the distance the cockatoos squabbled over which spot to spend the night and she heard a bat come past, but had not seen it. The bush had felt alive today; noisy and full of life. Every encounter seemed to point the way to this new transformation. Cockatoos for objectivity, cicadas for new life, kookaburra her spirit animal's presence was comforting and, as she was collecting firewood, she had frightened a skittish red-bellied black snake — as shy creatures who tend to be around when other more treacherous snakes are not, they are a symbol of good luck, fire energy and rebirth. Her intention was clear and it was time to begin.

She swept a large space in the cave clear of leaves and twigs, and made sure the place she planned to set her fire was safe. It would only be a small fire, just enough to stave off the mosquitoes and to give her light and fire for her ritual. More now than at any other time of year, she was vividly aware of the danger of a badly planned fireplace in the bush, but this was a well-worn fireplace and she trusted, with a little care, it would be just the right spot. She laid out the twigs and leaves for kindling and lay the larger branches to the side at the ready. In front of the fire she lay two dry grass tree sticks, one long and tapered at one end and the other split in half and notched along one edge, as well as a deep hollow shell and a small stringed bow. Tonight she would bring the fire to life herself, both within and without.

And so she began. She listened and looked around her, sitting quietly and still in the space, looking out from the cave's lip into the trees that grew in the valley below. She smelled the earthy scents of gum trees and native flowers. She heard the birds, and remembered the thump of the wallaby's feet bouncing through the trees as she made her way up the hill. 'Always moving forward,' she thought. She remembered all the animals she had encountered that day and wondered where they were right now. She looked out and saw a hollow in the branch of a tall tree and wondered who might live in there. She saw the sky's changing colors and felt the heaviness of the air drop a little with the cooling of the day. She looked to her fireplace, where many a fire would have been lit before and began her welcome:

I am the shelter of the cave
I am the awakening animals of the night
I am the summer songs of the birds
I am the roar of the cicadas
I am the deep dark blue of the sky
I am the longest day and the shortest night
I am the kookaburra who laughs
I am the fireplace of many

She sat in silence for a moment, soaking in the space fully and welcoming the spirits of place with her intention. She then rose and moved to the eastern side of the cave, and raising her hands said, 'May there be peace in the east.' She sent out a wave of love and compassion across the valley and out towards the ocean, thinking of all the people on boats, on islands and on the distant shores and lands of South America. She then turned to the northern side and said, 'May there be peace in the north,' envisioning all the people who lived in the land to the north, across the seas there, and in the entire northern hemisphere of the planet. Then to the west, 'May there be peace in the west,' and she saw in her mind's eye the expanses of desert and plains, farmlands and distant shores, more ocean and the far distant shores and lands of Africa. To the south she said, 'May there be peace in the south,' and let her mind see all the people and places to the south, the great southern oceans and the cold expanse of Antarctica. 'May there be peace. And may there be peace in all the worlds, the four corners of the world, and this world, the underworld and the otherworld. May there be peace.'

Feeling this peace within herself also, she returned to sit by the unlit fire. Speaking out loud, to make it feel real, she welcomed the spirits of the realms of land, sea and sky: 'I welcome the spirits of the land, the ground beneath me, the trees and plants and all beings who live in them. I welcome the spirits of the rocks, sand and dirt, and the great mass that is the planet. I welcome your energy as solidity, groundedness, stability, and strength. I honor your presence in my body as bone, tooth and muscle. Spirits of land, I give you thanks for the earth beneath my feet for without it, life would not be. Hail and welcome.

'I welcome the spirits of the sea, and all waters, the creeks, rivers, lakes, lagoons and the rain. I welcome the spirits of all water dwelling creatures. I welcome their energy as change, motion, fluidity, action and emotion. I honor your presence in my body as blood, spit and tears. Spirits of the Sea, I give you thanks, for without the waters of the world, life would not be. Hail and welcome.

'I welcome the spirits of the sky, the air, the weather, the sun, moon and stars. I welcome the spirits of all flying beings. I welcome your energy as swiftness, thought, consciousness and concept. I honor your presence in my breath and mind. Spirits of Air, I give you thanks, for without breath, life would not be. Hail and welcome.'

She then sat for a moment and thought of her ancestors and the long lines of lineage of which she was a part. She welcomed them: 'I welcome the ancestors and all who have gone before me. I welcome the ancestors of my bloodline, my culture, my people, my family; those who gave life for many generations, back to the beginning of life on earth. I welcome you and give thanks for my very being. For without you, I would not be. Hail and welcome.

'I welcome the ancestors of my inspirations, my teachers and guides and all who have brought me knowledge and led me to wisdom. You have shaped my mind and without your guidance, I would not be who I am today. Hail and welcome.

'I welcome the ancestors of this land, all those who have passed through here and the stories they left behind. I express my gratitude for your presence in this land and I wish your spirits well. I recognize the traditional owners and elders past and present, and wish the best for their people. Thank you for holding this space and keeping it safe for without you I would not be able to be here now. Hail and welcome.'

Part 2: Connecting with Nature

I will begin by sharing with you information that I have gathered and developed along with the people who come to the circles I run in Sydney. This includes a reworking of the idea of celebrating a wheel of the year as eight seasonal festivals to suit our local seasons, and sections exploring the symbolic meanings of local animals and plants. If you live in Sydney too it will hopefully be easy for you to recognize at least some of the seasonal patterns and animals listed here. If you live in another area of the country, or perhaps if you live in another part of the world, this section will serve as an example of what is possible to achieve when you set out to discover the energy and messages of your local area. Feel free to take what you connect with, let go of what you don't, and work towards developing a way of celebrating that works for you and helps you to connect to your own local sacred landscape. Let nature be your guide and, when in doubt, simply acknowledge and celebrate natural changes that are occurring in your area, keeping a record for next year.

The more you can take the time to step outside and feel into what is going on around you, the more you will learn, and the closer you will be to having a wheel of the year for your own area. This can take a number of years to develop, but it always begins with today.

Seasons and the Wheel of the Year

The wheel of the year is a system of eight equidistant seasonal celebrations throughout the year that is used by many modern Druids and neo-Pagans in their spiritual practice. Most of these festivals have their origins in pre-Christian practices of Pagan Britain and Ireland, but the idea of the full system of eight festivals is quite modern and seems to have first appeared in the 1950s. It may have originated with Gerald Gardner, who was the founder of modern Wicca, but at the same time Ross Nichols, who founded the Order of Bards Ovates and Druids (OBOD), began working with the idea in his group with variations on the names of the celebrations. Gerald and Ross knew each other and it is thought that they discussed ideas on this. With the increasing popularity of these modern traditions since that time, the system has become widely used as if from a single source. However, its origins are more complicated.

The wheel of the year consists of four 'solar festivals' of two solstices and two equinoxes, and four 'cross quarters', which fall in between the solar festival dates. The names of the cross quarters came from Celtic agricultural festivals and are still names of four months in the Irish calendar – Imbolc, Beltaine, Lughnassadh, and Samhain. Noticing the importance of the winter solstices in the layout of ancient burial tombs and also the winter solstice (Yule), summer solstice and the spring equinox in Anglo Saxon mythology, the solar festivals were added into a 'wheel' for the year along with a new addition of a festival at the autumn equinox (Mabon) to balance out the wheel and prevent a gap. Adding these to the cross quarter festivals, the result was an approximate six-week gap from one ritual to the next through the whole year.

The wheel of the year as an eight-spoked wheel of seasonal celebrations has become a widely accepted part of modern Druid and other Pagan practice. Even the autumn equinox has developed greater meaning as people have added harvest themes and worked in mythological connections. There is little to suggest that it was an important time for celebration for ancient people whether Celtic or Anglo Saxon. However, it is considered as important as any other festival on the wheel of the year as we now know it. The name for it, 'Mabon', was coined by Aidan Kelly in 1970, in reference to Mabon ap Modron, a character of the Welsh mythological collection called the Mabinogion. He also gave new names to the summer solstice as 'Litha' and to the spring equinox as 'Ostara', both words found in the Anglo-Saxon writing of Bede.

Despite the quite modern construction of this wheel of the year, I will be referring to it as the 'traditional wheel of the year' from here on in as it is the one most associated with traditional modern Paganism, as opposed to newer forms like those we are developing in Australian Druidry.

Many Pagans and Druids around the world celebrate the festivals of this traditional wheel of the year with seasonal

Traditional Wheel of the Year

decorations in their homes, with the sharing of old stories and myths, and with rituals that honor the ancestors as well as the land and its seasonal changes. It has proven a popular and potent way to align ourselves with the seasonal changes, taking time out of our daily lives to ground and recharge, as well as to give something back in the form of our acknowledgement, offerings, blessings and inspiration.

There are many ways that people work with the idea of the wheel of the year in Australia. Many Australian Druids work with this traditional wheel and the seasonal festivals of the northern hemisphere. Some celebrate them on the same dates as the northern tradition, feeling a connection to a global community of celebration and to the dates marked by their ancestors. Others switch the festival dates around by six months to account for the seasons being opposite here. In this way they enjoy the seasonal festivals as a myth of the agricultural cycle that maps out a journey for self-exploration through the year – the spring brings growth, the summer abundance, the autumn completion and the winter contemplation and rebirth. Many feel a connection with the non-native plants in their area as these continue to follow the traditional seasonal cycles. Some places, like Tasmania, even have similar growing seasons to the northern hemisphere and native deciduous trees, so this version of the wheel can make more sense there. Others, like myself, are exploring entirely new systems that reflect the unique seasonal changes in our parts of Australia, and at times working out how all these different versions of the wheel of the year might all work together in a synchronized whole.

Having spent much time in my life watching the seasonal changes and also trying to celebrate the traditional wheel's festivals, I have found that there are parts of the traditional celebrations that are relevant, but also there is a need for a new outlook. I have spent years taking a nature diary and making observations of the weather patterns, wind directions, ocean conditions, native plant flowering times and bird and animal behaviors. I collected these observations, shared them with like-minded friends and brainstormed how we could bring them into our rituals and perhaps blend them with the traditional seasonal festivals. We have done many experimental rituals – simply looking around us at what was happening in nature, trying to understand the symbolic meaning, considering the relevance to the traditional festivals and then learning how we can bring ourselves into alignment with that meaning through ritual.

We have celebrated the storms for helping us to unleash our wildness, the peacefulness of the first cool winds of autumn, the blooming of the wattle at the winter solstice reminding us that the sun is returning, the flowers at the awakening of spring bringing us inspiration and bringing new meaning to the story of the Goddess Brigid, the winds of the spring equinox encouraging us to bring about change and move into action, the shedding of the bark in early summer inspiring us to let go of what we don't need, and the bushfires of midsummer as a symbol of rebirth and remembrance of the sacredness of water. Sometimes we found patterns that occurred year after year; other times what happened one year would challenge us to rethink things the next year. We have had successes and failures, confusions and insights. We have struggled to fit the traditional wheel of the year festivals in where we can, found places where they fit perfectly, others where we had to let them go, and often there was a need for us to be open to some radical change. Sometimes we were able to incorporate the meaning of the traditional festivals, and at times both the northern and southern hemisphere versions could be relevant. We found that the exploration brought a depth of meaning to our rituals, and that the process of listening to the land and negotiating meaningful ways of celebrating was in itself the core of our practice. In the end, it all came down to allowing it to be a work in progress that we learn more from every time we come together to connect with the sacred landscape and celebrate the season, and we continue to do so.

There are no dates as the festivals we use are more periods of time than single dates. However, the solstices and equinoxes remain important times for peak and balance respectively and we often find these appropriate days for our rituals. Generally we celebrate them as we feel them arrive. Most of the time they do fall around about the time of the solstices, equinoxes and 'cross quarters' of the traditional wheel of the year, but our intuition should be our biggest guide. When I was studying with Morgan, my mentor in the UK, I remember noticing the cold and commenting that Samhain (31st October in the northern hemisphere) wasn't for a few weeks. She replied in a way that has stayed in my mind ever since. She explained that the timing of the festivals wasn't so much of a set date as a time you notice a shift. For her, Samhain was the day the winds came that blew the last of the brown leaves from the trees. That was what marked the shift. So it is with this in mind that I have steered away from set dates. Instead of expecting nature to work to our timetables, we learn to listen for when the season is ready to be celebrated. In developing a new wheel of the year, often we have needed to set aside our expectations, tune in with the energy of the land and celebrate what we feel. These are often the times we have learnt the most. Even as we learn more, however, this is a practice we should continue.

The land here often behaves in way that is less predictable than that of the lands of deciduous forests and there are significant differences of light through the year. The Australian bush is generally less concerned with the sun and light than it is with how much rain it is getting and what stage of the bushfire cycle it is in: some flowers don't care for seasons, they just come into bloom three weeks after a good downpour; some trees will only seed after a bushfire. In contrast to the easily identified seasons of spring growth, summer fruiting, autumn harvest and winter fallow of the northern hemisphere cycle, here in the native bushland at least there are two main times of growth – in the spring and autumn – and two times of 'death and rebirth' in the summer when the fires come, and in the winter in the darkness. Here, there are also the longer cycles of drought and rain, as well as bushfire and regrowth of the forest, which cycle over many years and decades.

It is not a simple thing to create a wheel of the year, and it takes much listening and learning. Looking to indigenous calendars has been useful for us in seeing this longer cycle and encourages us to keep on revising our wheel of the year, while still recording the experiences of previous years. We have found *D'harawal Seasons and Climatic Cycles* by Frances Bodkin (2008) to be most helpful, even though it outlines the seasons for the D'harawal region, which is in the west of Sydney. It helped to give us some ideas not only for the yearly wheel, but also introduced some ideas about longer cycles of hotter and cooler periods or times of more or less rain, that we are still learning about. You may find there are indigenous calendars that relate to an area near you that you can look to for some additional information. The more information we collect, the deeper we develop our wheel of the year and how we understand the seasons and their meanings. In the end it is not about creating a system and then always using that, no matter what happens around us. It is about sitting with nature and openly asking, 'What messages do you have for me in this moment, and how can I move into alignment with your energy?' That is a much more connected way of approaching the seasonal festivals. In the end, the wheel is just a guide.

A Wheel of Two Life Cycles

Before introducing the festivals individually, it needs to be mentioned that one major difference between our wheel and the traditional one is that we see our year's cycle as having two times of death and rebirth, not just one. This is a pretty new idea, but it works well for us. There is a complex story behind it, but to put it simply, in the traditional wheel of the year we see a story of the life cycle of the God as representative of the annual cycle of non-evergreen plants, along with the Goddess who represents the Earth. At mid-winter the God is 'born' from the Goddess, he grows to maturity through the spring and summer and is sacrificed in the autumn at the harvest. He is then born again at the following mid-winter solstice. This cycle is based on the growth of plants and their fruiting and fallow times throughout the year in the northern hemisphere. It is an agricultural cycle of planting, growth, harvest and storage.

It is plainly relevant in the lands where it came from, but here in Australia much of our bushland is evergreen, and in many places we can even grow vegetables right through the winter. In this sense, the traditional life cycle does not necessarily relate to either our native or agricultural cycles. In the first few years of running circles, we struggled over whether the summer solstice or winter solstice was the appropriate death time. Was death best represented by darkness, or by the bushfires? One Peace Festival, we brainstormed this idea and found we all resonated with introducing the idea that there are two symbolic deaths and rebirths creating a story of two life cycles. One is the death and rebirth of the sun at mid-winter solstice and the other is at mid-summer with the death and rebirth of the forest in the bushfires. One could argue this has some congruence with the traditional battle between the holly and oak kings, a Pagan story that overlaps the story of the God and Goddess. In that story the Oak

King represents the year between mid-winter and mid-summer as the weather warms and the plants grow. At summer solstice he battles the Holly King who will win and rule the land from mid-summer to mid-winter when they will battle again, with the Oak King winning. We have considered the relevance of this idea for us, but as these are both non-native species and we don't have any growing nearby, we have felt more connection with creating a new story.

This new story sees the journey of the year as an initiatory journey of two aspects of the self as a balance between light and dark. The light time from spring equinox to autumn equinox is active, outwardly focused, full of movement, action, determination and manifestation. The dark time from autumn equinox to spring equinox is more passive, reflective, introspective, metaphysical, and meditative. Through these halves of the year we see two life cycles emerge, beginning and ending at the

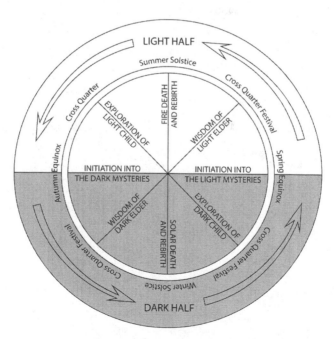

Year of Two Life Cycles

solstices, with a time of initiation into the mysteries at the equinox. We have also found these life cycle stories work well with our seasonal celebrations.

As an overview, there are two stories. They are based on the mysteries of light and dark as balancing principles that are within each of us. They are not terms meaning positive and negative or good and evil, but rather relate to our attention being either outward, active and in the physical world (light), or internal, reflective, contemplative, or spiritual (dark). One is the story of the dark child, born at winter solstice, who is initiated into the mysteries of the light at the equinox and ushered into action, bringing their intuitive wisdom out into the world. They mature into the light elder and gain proficiency and wisdom in their worldly action. This elder then dies in the fire time, letting go of associations with physical form, and finding new insight to be reborn into another life cycle as the light child. This light child is wild and exuberant, fully of life and energy. They see the world with fresh eyes and their energy needs to be danced and expressed until the initiation into the mysteries of the dark at the autumnal equinox where they learn to temper that energy and look within. This looking within and finding stillness and wisdom brings them to maturity as the dark elder and they gain proficiency in exploring the inner worlds. This elder then dies and is reborn again as the dark child at the winter solstice. The dark child is full of inner wisdom, inspiration and wonder. They see their inner world through fresh eyes and develop ideas that will be initiated into action at the equinox. Each of the seasonal festivals in our wheel of the year helps to tell the story of these two life cycles in greater fullness.

The life cycle stories help us to see the festivals as a complete story. They help us to see the projects and learning in our lives as relating to the world around us. As the world is in the dark time, so too are we. We become more introspective and internally focused. When the world is in the light time we are more active and outwardly focused. At the times of initiation we need to adjust our focus and move into the different energy. Looking at the year in this way can help us to understand both nature and ourselves better and bring balance to our lives.

Rebirth

Feeling the twilight edge towards darkness, it was time to begin the fire starting. She touched her amulet and, closing her eyes, asked for its help in bringing in the fire energy. She set up the bow with the cord wrapped around the long grass tree stalk, then placed the upper end in the shell and the lower end onto the notched board. Taking a deep breath she moved the bow slowly back and forth, putting pressure on the shell to hold the stick in place and create friction. It was a long process at times and she would have to be patient. Slowly, the friction let out a little sawdust from the notch, dropping onto a leaf she had set in place there. Then she began to pick up the pace. 'Come on,' she said under her breath, 'let's see that glow baby.' It didn't happen on the first try, or the second. Frustrated, she looked over at her backpack. There was a lighter in there... 'No,' she said out loud, 'I want it to come from me,' and took up the fire sticks again. 'Third time lucky, hey?' she asked them and with a deep breath, began again. She smelt the smoke before she saw it, it was such a small wisp, but as she continued she started to be able to see it, even in the dim light. More smoke, and she felt her arms beginning to fade, 'No... let's go,' she said and put in an extra push, back and forth, back and forth the bow ground the stick down. The dust started to come out blackened...and then there it was: the tiny pinprick of a glow on the dust.

She excitedly got down to cup the leaf in her hands and blow the heat of the spark onto the rest of the dust. As it lit, she continued to blow softly and reached for the clump of stringy bark she'd kept handy for nesting the coal into. She put it inside and covered it over gently, then blew on it again, hoping this would be her first time getting it going all by herself. It felt so much better to bring the fire to life through her own efforts, as though her own inner fire was transferred into the coal. She blew again and through the smoke she could see the coal was still glowing red. Blow, breathe, blow, breathe. Then it caught alight. The flame had arrived. Quickly she put it into her stack of kindling and adjusted the twigs to be in place to catch fire more easily, and once they did, she began putting the thicker sticks of wood onto the fire.

As she got into the motions of building her little fire, she quietly began chanting, 'Awen.' She took a long deep breath, and on the outbreath sounded out the word long and strong. She felt each sound as a vibration in her body. As she sounded the 'Ahhhhh' she felt her connection to the earth, as she sounded 'Ooooo' she felt the wateriness of her belly and her womb, with the 'Ehhhhh' she felt her breath, throat and lungs and with 'Nnnnnn' her head seemed to vibrate right on her forehead with an intensity like fire. It was as though she was bringing all the elements into her body, but it was also an awakening of the life force, the energy that animates, and the energy that brings about inspiration, blessings and art; the energy of Awen.

She stared at the flames of the fire as she intoned it and remembered feeling it at her first circle. The ritual leader had offered all new members of the circle to come to the centre and be initiated by the Awen chant. This would ignite the Awen within them, so that their poetry and art could begin to flow. She stood in the centre of the circle with two other new initiates, as the gathering chanted 'Awen' three times around them in beautiful harmony. She closed her eyes and felt the sound of it wash over her. Afterwards she was told that now she had been initiated, at the next circle she would be invited to be a part of the eisteddfod. 'What's an eisteddfod?' she had asked the older lady standing beside her in the circle. 'You'll see,' and a sly smile was all she got as a reply. Indeed, the next part of the circle had been the eisteddfod and she was impressed to see the talented Bards entertain them all with their music, poems and funny stories about the season. Everyone was welcome and encouraged to have a go, and some new members who had been initiated at the last festival were invited to share what they had been learning. One bravely shared a shaky tin whistle song and ended it with a shy smile that was greeted with warm encouragement and thanks. Another *offered a rhyming poem that brought out a few giggles, raised eyebrows and nods of approval from the more experienced Bards.*

She laughed a little to herself. That one had been a natural Bard long before his initiation. She, on the other hand, had struggled to break out of her own fears of what other people would think, worried that what she did wouldn't be good enough. She'd been working on that all year and had learnt a lot, both about herself and about her art. She'd chosen to learn to drum. She loved the energy and vibrancy of it, and felt alive when joining in a drumming circle or with other musicians, but she found it hard to get to the point where she could let go. She knew that it was when she let go that the Awen flowed strongest for her – when she just went with the rhythm of something inside her, like a dance, and stopped worrying about what others thought. But that was easier said than done.

The fire was strong now. Not large, but holding its flame well enough. The smoke was sweet and its presence quickly dissuaded the lurking insects to hang around. She gazed at the flames and contemplated the meaning of the festival as a rebirthing. What did this mean for her? It was the time of year when she and her regular circle of friends felt that the 'light elder' dies to be reborn as the 'light child'. 'What do I need to let go of?' she wondered out loud, 'And what am I moving into?'

As she looked to the flames she thought about all she had learned in this year and this life. All the wisdom that had come her way, through wise teachers, kind parents, good friends, inspiring stories and heartfelt song lyrics. Even the hard times and difficult relationships had been great teachers. What she had learned about the world and her place in it had come from so many sources it was hard to comprehend. Looking at the flames she watched twigs that were once part of trees shrivel, bend, blacken and turn to ash and smoke. 'Nothing ever stays the same. There's always something else to come.' She felt thankful for the light and the smoke. 'What is yet to come? What old me am I letting go of? And what new me am I going to find?'

She thought of the meaning of the Fire Festival. She felt lucky at being able to be here in the bush in a mild year, and to feel real fire before her without threat. When the bushfires came, this festival was powerful in a whole other way. Everyone felt it then. It was all people could talk about. All over the news were interviews with people who had lost their homes and all their belongings. Every time they say the same thing. 'At least we all got out okay,' they say. And if someone was lost, no one ever cared about their TVs anymore. The fires always made people aware of what was really important. It's not stuff. It's not our house or our job or our trophies or our money, or any of those things. The only thing that matters is that we are here to experience the world with each other. Given half an hour's notice that the fires are coming people might think to grab some sentimental things...photos, journals, letters, but with five minutes... Thirty seconds... Ten seconds... It quickly becomes clear what's really important: just life. 'Nothing else matters,' she thought, 'just...life. Just being here now, to experience all this...'

The Coastal Sydney Wheel of the Year

The image created for this wheel moves in an anticlockwise direction. This is because in the southern hemisphere the arc of the sun's position in the sky begins in the east and swings to the north before setting in the west. In the northern hemisphere it swings to the south, making a clockwise movement. This is not a new idea. Indeed it is also known as 'sunwise' making reference to the differences we experience in the two hemispheres. I have often wondered how it might be practiced on the equator however! If you live in the tropics, you may have to feel into what works for you, or perhaps there is a better way? It's all a part of the exploration. Let the Earth be your guide.

The following seasons are drawn as eight equidistant seasons, but are more like seasons that overlap or last different lengths of time in different years. Some years a season might come in a

Coastal Sydney Wheel of the Year

39

jumbled order or the weather might be changeable and skip around. All of this is not 'wrong'. Nature is never wrong. We just need to adjust to feel into what it is speaking to us. These seasonal festivals act as a guide to what may be going on, and some ideas about how to symbolically work with that. But, when gathering for ritual, the best thing to do is always to build onto what exists with further inquiry, to deepen our practice and bring us into closer connection with nature. The festivals then evolve further.

Fire Festival

Meaning: Death, rebirth, cleansing, purification, clear vision, recognition of what is truly important

Time period: Late November to late February – can overlap with both Barkfall and/or Storm festivals, though celebrated either at the summer solstice or in January

Elements: Fire and water

Colors: Red, yellow, orange and black

Plants: Christmas bush, frangipani, dry leaves and bark

Solar cycle: Height of power before time of decline

Ocean cycle: Warm waters. Generally clean waves in the morning, choppy waves from about 10am

Wind cycle: North-easterly especially after noon

Life cycle: Death of the light/active elder and rebirth of the light/active child

This time is marked by hot dry days and often a high threat of bushfire. The fires in Australia are a very important part of the life cycle of the forest. Many Australian plants will not release their seeds unless they reach temperatures over 180 degrees Celsius. The fires literally bring death and rebirth to the forest, and in recognizing them as an important part of the natural cycle, we can bring that energy into our practice and explore what it means for us as we move into alignment with it.

The fires renew and refresh the forest. They burn away what is no longer necessary and make way for new growth. They eliminate all the junk and mess of leaf litter and Barkfall. They burn it all away and by doing so open up the forest to new growth and new life. This we can see as a rebirth and an initiation by fire. The stripping away of everything that is unnecessary. We can honor this energy and bring it into our lives by considering what it is we need to let go of and what we have become attached to. It encourages us to be minimalist, strip back what we don't need and allow for new growth to thrive in us.

Taking time to contemplate the very real threat of bushfires to human lives can also be a powerful part of this festival. The fires remind us of how easily all we have can be taken away from us. The power of nature can sweep through, turning all our belongings to ash and rubble so quickly. Thinking about what would happen if the fires were to come to our home, we learn to become aware of what is really important, what we could not live without. This becomes a contemplation on the true self, the nature of life, identity and letting go of the physical. These are all part of the journey of death and rebirth for the light elder who moves into the next phase as the light child. The symbolic light elder within each of us must face the potential destruction of all they have built in this world, all the action they have made, all that they have created, all the identity they may be clinging to. To be reborn, they must allow for this to be burned away in the element of fire and learn to see the world with fresh eyes. They recognize that the true self is so much more than a collection of belongings or identities. The true self is one with nature and what will still be there when the light child is born. We certainly don't need to burn all our belongings to realize this, but instead we will use meditation or symbolic activities like home clearing to express this journey.

Water is often an important element in this ritual for us. It is in the heat of the year that we face the threat of drought most greatly and water is at its scarcest. It also helps save our homes from destruction in fire-fighting. I have often focused my rituals in the Fire Festival on the powers of water. Certainly, it is not a good idea to bring fire into the outdoor ritual space when there are fire bans in place, nor is it legal. Holding a ritual that involves a swim or a dunk in some cool water, or sharing a drink of fresh cold water can help us to honor this time as being when balance is also needed.

We should note that some years we get a lot of rain over summer and the weather stays mild, particularly in the La Nina cycle. These years the threat of fire is low and the focus of the festival activities in these instances changes. In these years our celebrations would centre on gratitude for having been spared the threat, and recognition of the unique elements of this difference, though we may still journey with the light elder into a symbolic rebirth. One year we noticed an abundance of spiders and birds as a result of the increased rain, so we considered the symbolic meaning of this as a time to share our dreams and brought that into our ceremony as well. The most important thing is to listen and create ceremonies that help us to move into alignment with the energy of the land.

Storm Festival

Meaning: Fertility, growth, birth, new life, love and lust, wildness, emotions, new projects, expression, release through movement
Timing: Mid-January to early March
Elements: Water and wind
Colors: Bright green, blue and black
Plants: Fresh new growth after bushfires; melaleuca flowers
Solar cycle: Retreat of the sun to the north
Ocean cycle: Warm waters; choppy waves; storms bring calm

oceans

Wind cycle: North-easterly, with southerlies bringing churning storms after hot days

Life cycle: The exploration of the light child in the world

A time of new life, fertility, rain, energy, and new growth. As the wind starts to swing towards the south, the hot humid days often end with dramatic storm fronts, lightning shows and torrential downpours. These afternoon winds from the south carry the ominous message that summer will soon be coming to an end. The air is thick and heavy with humidity. If the fires have come this year, the burnt trees begin to grow fresh shoots from their trunks and seeds will start to germinate in the ashes. Grass trees will sprout new growth quickly and the land will be all black, white and bright green in those places.

The water and fire elements energy of this time of year are strong even in years when there is less rain. This energy leaves people feeling emotional, exasperated and stressed, and in deep need of energetic release. As a result, the storms at this time are certainly the best for dancing in. This is the energy of the light child, who we often refer to as the 'tempest child'. Within us we feel her/his energy and frustration, a need for release and for wildness. It is a great time of year to indulge the inner child. To bring into our lives more exploration, play, dance, fun, messy art and expression. Jump in puddles, dance in the rain, play in the mud. Get to know the world like a child would, in every messy corner. This is a youthful time for both us and the land. We are in a phase of new growth after the oppressive heat of mid-summer; the storm energy brings us a feeling of needing to express ourselves and to be vibrant and full of fertile creativity. In our lives the fresh eyes of the light child help us to see what is truly important. The fires have left us knowing what this is. It is our connection with others, our creativity and our joy of life. This is what we celebrate here.

We should note that some years the storms are not as potent as they are other years. Some years the drought stops the rains for months. Sometimes the storm fronts come, but no rain falls. Despite this, we can often still feel the energy of the light child. It's the end of the hot part of the year and we tend to feel restless and emotional even if there is no rain to allow us to cool off. Taking time in ritual to explore how this has been making us feel can be soothing and bring us insight, and we have often taken this festival as a time to share our struggles and find ways of expressing them in our rituals.

Peace Festival

Meaning: Peacefulness, meditation, calming, moving inwards, reflection, contemplation

Timing: Around the autumn equinox (March 22), mid-March to late April

Elements: Wind and earth

Colors: White, pale blue, pale pink, pale green

Plants: Grevillea

Solar cycle: Balance of heat and cold

Ocean cycle: Beginning to cool; less choppy waves

Wind cycle: Cooling, but not yet cold. Starting to come more from the south, but balanced

Life cycle: Initiation into the darkness for the light child. They learn the mysteries of the dark and move into their role as the dark adult

The storms become gentler rain as the humidity subsides and the dry air from the southwest blows in. The air becomes cool and fresh and the world seems generally quieter. The water is still warm in the ocean, but it's noticeably beginning to cool down. The temperature seems comfortable, gentle, safe and peaceful. It's a time when you might gladly reach for a jumper for the first time or notice your skin feels cooler. We often notice around this time that there are fewer flies, ants and mosquitoes about, there's less need for the sunscreen, and it's more comfortable to be outside generally. The elements of fire and water that brought so much emotion and stress to us in the storm season are subsiding and becoming more balanced.

This is a great time for rituals that reflect this peacefulness and calm. We often include meditation, contemplation, share thoughtful poetry, or do other quiet activities. Our emotional state from the last ritual seems soothed completely by the time this ritual swings around; if it isn't, we work on using the energy of the time to find our way there.

The initiation of the light child into the dark mysteries is also important in this festival. This can take the form of contemplation on the inner worlds, meditation, and learning practices to observe the inner state. It can also be a time when we dedicate ourselves to a path of learning and self-improvement. The dark half of the year is a time for the inner self. We look within to improve our understanding of our inner nature. We might take up a daily meditation practice, explore a series of mythologies, learn to write poetry, or study a new Druidic concept. Learning and contemplation are a focus of our energy for the whole of the dark half of the year. We focus in these rituals much more on the self and the inner world, the mysteries of the otherworld and encounters with spirit. This festival is an initiation for us all into working with that energy.

Interestingly, this festival often sits well with the popular festival of Easter and its timing. The celebration of new life is not so out of place as it seemed when we followed the traditional calendar, as we know that this is one of two important times of growth in the natural cycle of the bush. It is also a time for us to grow in new ways, working within for greater self-understanding.

Moon Festival

Meaning: Ancestors and spirit communication, divination, magic, mysteries, psychic work

Timing: Early May to mid-June

Elements: Earth and water

Colors: White, black, silver, purple

Plants: She oak

Solar cycle: The nights are lengthening

Ocean cycle: Clean glassy waves. Water still cooling

Wind cycle: Begins to blow cold from the south west, off the mountains

Life cycle: Maturation of the dark adult into the dark elder

As the sun sinks further to the northern horizon and the days grow shorter, a chill can be felt in the air. The wind now often comes from the south-west blowing crisp, clean air from the mountains. Some years this wind blows away the humidity and leaves vast clear skies, other years it brings relentless rain and sometimes flooding. When visible, the moon is bright in the night skies as it rises full for the first time of the year in darkness. The darkness is upon us now and we feel a movement towards more indoor activity. We notice the dark sneaking in earlier each evening and helping us to turn inwards more and more.

This time coincides beautifully with the Samhain festivities of the traditional wheel of the year and we find they share many ritual aspects. The life cycle story has the dark adult maturing into the dark elder. We explore this through the use of divinatory tools such as oracle cards or ogham, or taking an oracle walk, deep meditation, discussing and incorporating magical aspects into our rituals, and/or journeying meditation often involving spirit guides or ancestors. Through these activities we learn about our 'dark side': our hidden or subconscious self. We don't see the 'dark' part of ourselves as 'bad' in any sense, but rather it is the self of our thoughts, dreams and meditations. It is the part of us that speaks in symbols and mystery. It can relate to that which we hide from ourselves. This can be negative in some sense, such as our guilt, pain, loss, worry, doubt or fear, but through practices of self-exploration we work to delve into these parts of ourselves, unpack them, love them, and work with them to find the gifts they can bring us and our community. This is a time of great transformation and magical working.

The moon itself is important to all of these elements of our rituals. The moon is a representation of 'seeing in the dark'. She is the symbol of the dark half of the year, the Goddess, the passive, the feminine, the mystery. The moon's light is a reflection of the sun. Similarly, at this time of year we contemplate all we have achieved in the light half of the year, and reflect upon it in our meditation in order to bring greater understanding to our actions in the next cycle.

Descending into the darkness of winter we also reflect on the journey to death and take time to honor our ancestors. Often during the ritual for this festival we take some time to recall stories of our lost loved ones and connect with our ancestral histories as individuals and as a group.

Hardening Festival

Meaning: Working on inner strength and inner wisdom, learning, study, community, the home, storytelling, music, sharing, feasts

Timing: Around the winter solstice (June 21-22), from early to mid-June to the end of July

Elements: Earth and fire

Colors: Dark colors and wattle yellow

Plants: Golden wattle

Solar cycle: The sun starts its return

Ocean cycle: Clean, offshore blown waves or southerly wild

waves; cold water
Wind cycle: South-westerly and cold
Life cycle: The dark elder dies and is reborn as the dark child

The wind and air has turned cold and the days are at their shortest. With the cold south-westerly winds blowing, the native trees' trunks are hardening and thickening to protect their inner layers. We too are bracing ourselves, putting on more layers of clothing and we might notice the first days in June that we feel like wearing gloves. Our focus has turned from outward activity to indoor activities of learning, poetry and the home. It is a great time for getting stuck into our studies and working with the 'dark' as the world of concepts and ideas. It's also a great time for working with spirit as Awen for learning new creative expressions, particularly for the purpose of entertainment and sharing as this is a time when community, talking, storytelling and music are the light in our world.

It's a time when we need to find a balance between our tendency to become introverted and draw within, and our need to balance this with social activity. Even though in many parts of Australia the dark time is still quite light in comparison to the experiences of our northern hemisphere counterparts, it's still a time when many people experience depression of SADS (Seasonal Affective Disorder Syndrome). We can transform this feeling from sadness to joy with a ritual based on community and sharing myths, poems, songs and stories, a good fire, and a nice hearty feast, and perhaps a chance to wear a Druid cloak.

In the story of the life cycles, this is the time when the dark elder is reborn as the dark child. The wisdom gained in self-exploration and study often leads us to renewed ideas about who we are and how we think about ourselves. The dark elder time of the Moon Festival helped us to delve deep into ourselves and see our true nature more clearly from within as we explored our 'dark side'. We have gained insight about our life's purpose through this exploration and the initiation of this festival sees us re-birthing ourselves into that new purpose. We let go of old behaviors and thought patterns, and come into new ways of seeing and being. At the summer solstice, the death of the light elder and rebirth of the light child had us consider letting go of parts of our external reality to find our true self. This was an external, physical, active, worldly rebirth. In contrast, the death of the dark elder and rebirth of the dark child is more about a letting go of that which we no longer need in our inner reality. This can be unnecessary thought forms, identity stories and concepts. Letting these go we come to find the true self in another way.

An important symbol for us at this time of year is the wattle, as it comes into bloom in abundance here very close to the winter solstice. Particularly the golden wattle (*Acacia longifolia*), which has a long yellow bloom rather than the globe shape. To us it represents the rays of light from the sun that will continue to grow in strength from this time on. It also represents Awen and the creative arts. These flowers and many other flowers will continue to appear in abundance until the next festival.

Flower Festival

Meaning: Inspiration, creativity, joy, youthfulness, beauty, awakening, expressiveness

Timing: Early August to mid-September (may happen either side of Wind Change if that festival comes early)

Elements: Air and earth

Colors: bright and pastel colors – red, pink, purple, yellow, orange, green

Plants: All wildflowers, but particularly boronia, crowea and many varieties of wattle

Solar cycle: The sun is gaining strength. The days grow longer

Ocean cycle: Water still cold and clear

Wind cycle: South-westerly and still cold

Life cycle: The exploration of the dark child in the world.

Many Australian wildflowers bloom at this time of the year and it is a wonderful season for bushwalking and spending time finding inspiration in nature. In much of Australia there is no time when flowers are completely absent, but certainly this time of year has an abundance of flowers in our area, especially in coastal heathlands on the tops of the hills. Flowers are a symbol of beauty, youthfulness, fertility, joy, and creativity. We have found this festival works beautifully with the traditional festival of Imbolc as being sacred to the Goddess Brigid. Brigid is the Goddess of poets, inspiration and crafts. At this time we tend to focus our rituals on the raising of Awen through sharing music, poetry and dedicating ourselves to our arts in their many forms. We sing to the land to help it awaken from the cold, we use drumming and other instruments to bring in the spring and shake up the lands energy after the sleepy time of winter. In contrast to the storytelling of the Hardening Festival when the focus was on community and sharing in a time of darkness, now is a time of awakening new ideas within ourselves and becoming seekers of inspiration. We dedicate ourselves to new learning and asking for greater inspiration in what we do.

It's a great time for the first outdoor ritual after it being cold for so long and we often take a bushwalk to see the wildflowers, or to a beautiful place to have a picnic and have our ritual. It's one of the most comfortable times of year for walking and getting outside and moving feels really good.

In the story of the life cycles this is the time of the dark child. The dark child is a symbol of the innate wisdom we all have. Connecting with the purity and innocence of our inner child is a potent pathway to finding our creativity and joy. After stripping away our mental baggage in the rebirth at the Hardening, we find ourselves open to new ideas, new inspirations, and new creative thinking. We are getting inspired for the action that is to come with the light half of the year, but right now we are in the stage of preparation, inspiration and creative thinking.

Wind Change Festival

Meaning: Manifestation, action, change, movement, putting ideas into action

Timing: Begins sometime between mid-August and mid-September, and ends around mid-to late-October

Elements: Air and water

Colors: Yellow and pink; then purple and grey

Plants: Globe wattle, bottlebrush and jacaranda

Solar cycle: Hot days intersperse with the cold; days may be up to 30 degrees Celsius

Ocean cycle: Water still cold, but the air is warm, so it's often a time for the first swim

Wind cycle: Alternates between southern cold winds and western or northerly hot winds

This period could be broken up into two sections. The first dry and warm, the second cooler and wetter. Beginning sometime around the end of August to the end of September, the wind moves from the south-west where it has blown from most of the winter, around to the north and north east where it will blow from for most of summer. In the transition we get a few weeks when the winds often blow from the west and north-west and bring a period of warmer-than-usual dry sunny days. It seems like summer has come early. Yet this is just the interim time between the cold dry and the warm humid seasons of the year. The end of this time is usually marked by another change to cooler days again and more humidity and rain as the winds start to become more northern and north-easterly. The jacaranda trees bloom purple across the city and the rainy days can be relentless, at times raining for a week or more on end. The jacarandas will continue to bloom into the next festival.

Some years these two sections are distinct and quite clearly separate, and other years they blend into one long and rather moody season of changeability in the weather with temperatures sometimes swinging ten to fifteen degrees from one day to the next as the wind makes up its mind about which direction to blow from. We also tend to get a lot of days with strong winds and often rough seas and big swells. Whatever transpires, there is a strong feeling of change in the air. It's a time when we need to be adaptable and on our toes, ready for anything.

For many people this is the time they first get in the water for the summer season, yet although the air is warm, the water is still cold. This is a great time to celebrate on the beach or near other waterways, to honor the ocean and ocean deities and stories like those of Manannan and Lir, to ask for protection in the water and to bless those at sea, and to remember those who have died at sea. We can also honor the role of the ocean and the waters as a space of healing, particularly as we come into the hotter time of the year, when it will be used by many as an escape from the heat.

The changeable nature of this time of the year makes it a good time to think about change in our own lives. To do the spring cleaning, move house, get a new job, or start a new exercise regime. It's a time of freshening, but also a time of coming into action. We are now in the light half of the year. At this festival we explore the story of the dark child being initiated into the mysteries of the light. The inner contemplation and inspired ideas and creativity found in the dark time now need to be manifested into physical form through action, movement and change. This is a great time to ask, 'What change do I want to see in the world, and how can I be that change?' It is a good time to dedicate ourselves to charitable activity, or activism of some kind, supporting a movement that moves us! We might even consider what movement we can bring into our own personal lives through doing more physical activity, taking up a sport for the summer, or creating a new exercise routine. It's all about movement, change and action.

Barkfall Festival

Meaning: Work, shedding, organizing, testing, omens and signs, ending of studies, celebration
Timing: Mid-November to mid-December
Elements: Fire and earth
Colors: Brown, purple and red
Plants: Jacaranda and bottlebrush, fallen bark from scribbly gums and Sydney red gums
Solar cycle: Days get hotter and noticeably longer
Ocean cycle: Water is warming and becomes more choppy
Wind cycle: Starts to blow more from the north, bringing humidity and cloudy days

The beginning of this period is noticeable by the day it gets hot enough for the trees to begin cracking and shrugging off their bark and leaves in heaping piles. The bark that had kept them insulated and protected through the winter is shed, making them cooler, but also creating some tinder that will encourage the burning to come at the Fire Festival. We too tend to do some natural shedding at this time. We start wearing less clothing, or shorter sleeves, pants or skirts. If we started an exercise regime at Wind Change we will be starting to see the first shedding of some winter weight as we find our bodies adjust to the change of season.

This time also coincides with many end-of-year activities, from final exams for those studying, to wrapping up the work year before the Christmas and New Year break. There are a lot of parties, BBQs, family get-togethers and the like. It's a time when everyone is busy and life is incredibly social and a lot of fun. It also means we need to take time out sometimes to balance this. The same as we needed extra social stimulation in winter, now we need to create balance by spending time alone. In more ways than one, our regular life and routines go out the window to accommodate all this activity. Like the trees letting go of their bark, we let go of the regularity of our daily lives, making way for some refreshing time out to come in the New Year with a holiday break and the Fire Festival to come.

The jacarandas blooming can occur in either this time or the rainy time that happens as a part of the Wind Change Festival. When they bloom it always seems to coincide with a period when many of us have noticed more synchronicities, chance meetings, seeing omens and signs or other significant messages from spirit. These messages seem to come in the physical world more often than in dreams, as though this is the light half of the year's version of what we experienced at the Moon Festival. And as the Moon Festival related to Samhain, this time coincides with Beltaine. In the traditional wheel of the year these are the times where the veils between the worlds are thin, meaning it is a good time for divination, communication with spirits and nature and working with ancestral energy. There is a balance between the two also. While Moon Festival was a recognition of death, now is a time to recognize life and its wonderful gifts.

Keeping a Nature Diary

One of the best ways to connect to the natural cycles around you and work towards creating your own local wheel of the year is to regularly take note of the changes you see and to make a record of them in a nature diary. In this way you can begin to see patterns emerging that will give you insights as to how to lead your life and be in tune with the world around you.

There are a few areas in which you should begin to take note of change. You may find that you actually have a good understanding of these cycles already, but that you have never ordered them into any kind of system. Through keeping records you will be able to see patterns in the changes and to map out a cycle that you can use as a base for your own local wheel of the year, and then your own series of rituals that correspond with these, bringing you deeply in tune with the place in which you live.

You might be dedicated enough to make a record every day for a year, but this can be tiresome, particularly when conditions stay the same over a period of time. What can work better is to create a few worksheets, as well as a weekly or fortnightly diary entry that you can stick to, that will fill out over a number of years. Yes, this is a project that will require a bit of patience, or perhaps a lifetime of listening, but that is what being a part of a living tradition is about and you are creating valuable information for those who will come after you. Don't forget to share what you learn.

You should keep both accounts of changes you notice in detail and also an overview of the year as a wheel that you can look at as a whole. Keep a notebook for this. At the front draw a circle and mark four points to represent the solstices and equinoxes. The rest of the spaces can come into form as you recognize times of change. To begin with you might add a few notes to this wheel, but only if you are confident of the patterns. Otherwise, leave it blank until you have more notes. Each time you notice a change in the weather, such as strong winds, periods of rain, a change in the growth of plants, or blooming of flowers, or simply the mood of the season, start a new page and fill out some points. These might include:

Date:
Weather:
Temperature:
Wind direction and feeling:
Colors I've noticed in nature:
Flowers blooming:
Animal behaviors:
Plant growth:
Ocean's mood and wind (onshore/offshore):
Feeling of the season:
My emotional state:
What I'm feeling drawn to doing:
Notes on season's meaning:

Fill out as much or as little as you want to each time. Some times of year will come through to you easily. Others might take a bit of time to contemplate and see how they work with the rest of the year. In the section marked 'Notes on season's meaning' contemplate what the symbols of the season are and how you could understand them for your own personal development. Learning more about elemental correspondences, animal and plant symbols, numerology, mythology or other pathways can help to broaden your interpretations.

You can keep a list in your notebook of things you would like to look out for. For example, when does the bark begin to fall? When does this or that plant come into flower? What season do you see this bird in the area, and is there a time when they leave? When are the birds nesting or territorial? What are the times of highest rainfall, or greatest threat of fire? You could also consider local agricultural activity if you live in an area where this is a part of your environment, or the harvest times in your own garden. Creating a list reminding you to keep an eye out for these things will help you to notice them when they come.

Once you have a few changes noted, preferably with a year's observations, it's time to start creating the overview for your wheel. You may not need a whole year of notes, however, as you might have enough information from the top of your head if you have been noticing changes without keeping a diary. I found I had a lot of memories of the weather through my life when I started to think about it. Turning back to your wheel page, it is now time to start filling in the details from your notes and memories. Working around the circle, abbreviate your ideas as concisely as you can and note key points. Think about words that encapsulate the feeling of the season or important symbols. What is the strongest symbol you noticed at that time? Can you name a section of your year after that symbol? Alternatively, perhaps you could draw images or color the section to have the feeling of that time of year. Make the process creative and find your own way to explore the expression of the season.

Over time, perhaps many years, your wheel will begin to take form as a whole. It may change a little each year also. You will see different aspects of the seasons and learn more about them each time the wheel turns. If what you noticed last year doesn't happen this year, don't worry, you didn't get it wrong, you are simply deepening your understanding as you learn more. As this happens you will also be able to incorporate a bit more depth into your ritual practice, adding new ideas for contemplation and filling out the complexity of the year's story. I can't stress enough: don't be afraid of getting it wrong. So long as you are listening to the land and looking to find the wisdom of the trees and nature, you're on the right track. Be aware too that it will never be finished, just as the cycles of seasons are never finished, but move through endless cycles of renewal and gradual change. See this work rather as a constant practice that you will always be deepening; at all times make nature your guide over what is written on the page.

If you choose to create rituals to celebrate what you've noticed in the seasons, keep a record of these also, with notes on what you did, how it went, what worked well, and what didn't work so well. There are no mistakes, only opportunities to learn.

Animal Symbolism

In modern Druidry animal symbolism is a popular subject. Many of the myths and legends feature animals and characters often shapeshift into animal form. Many spiritual lessons come from interacting not only with spirit forms of animals, but also with actual animals in the wild. Seeing an animal in the wild is often seen as an omen we can interpret as having significance to our life's journey. When I first started learning about Druidry and Paganism more generally, I would come across books that dealt with the symbolic meanings of animals, but of course, the animals most often spoken of would be the wolf, bear, fox, boar, bull, swan, eagle, cat and raven as these were the ones that appeared in the stories. No one mentioned the significance of the wombat, cockatoo, kangaroo or goanna, and why would they? Thankfully, however, there are now various resources for finding this kind of information. In Australian Indigenous traditional stories there are many things we can learn about native animals, and there are also resources like *Gondwana Dreaming* by Anja-Karina Pahl, a book that specifically describes the symbolic nature of many native animals from an Indigenous perspective. There are also oracle card decks such as the *Animal Dreaming Oracle* cards by Scott Alexander King that work with Australian animal symbolism and various tarot decks that can be useful.

More importantly we can gain much understanding of the symbolic relevance of any animal by simply looking at their nature and observing their behaviors, habitats, and physical forms. I recommend buying a good set of field guides. I have one each for birds, mammals, reptiles and fish and in each of them I put a mark in each time I see an animal and take note of its behaviors both in my seeing it and in the book. These help me to work out the symbolic meaning. By interpreting their nature directly, we no longer need reference books. Nature speaks for itself. Here are some examples from my own observations:

Koala

The name 'koala' means 'no water' as koalas do not need to drink and get all the moisture they need from eucalyptus leaves. As a result they represent resourcefulness, adaptability and survival. They spend much of their time drowsy or asleep, so they represent inner journeys, dreaming and meditation. They are also quite noisy at mating time, making them a symbol of passion, but also of anger and jealousy.

Kangaroo

The image of the big red kangaroos with their muscled chests, fighting for their rank and right to mate, represents the kangaroo's magical symbolism in strength, power, protection and masculine energy. Their legs do not allow them to move backwards, so they also represent progression, travel, endurance and moving on.

Wombat

Living in underground burrows and coming out in the night, wombats are a symbol of homely comforts, home-making, homesickness, and stability. With their thick, stout bodies they represent standing your ground, self-confidence and security. The energy of the wombat is of reliability, responsibility, study and family life.

Kookaburra

The cackling call of the kookaburra is a familiar sound over much of Australia, sounding much like a hearty laugh they represent humor and looking on the bright side of life. As they are often heard laughing before storms they represent weather knowledge, storm energies, insight, divination and prophecy.

Platypus

Platypus both lays eggs and gives milk to its young, so represents women's mysteries, duality, mysteries of childbirth, and motherhood. They also defy the categories of mammal and bird, and so are a symbol of the unexpected and paradoxical, thresholds, mysteries of evolution and progression, adapting to new situations, and changing to suit our environment.

Lyre Bird

The tail feathers of the lyre bird look like the lyre, a kind of harp. They are adept copycats and learn to sing the songs of many other birds as well as other sounds around them. They have been known to imitate chainsaws, traffic sounds and phone ringtones. They are an unmistakable symbol of the Bard, musician and entertainer, as well as the impersonator, actor and shapeshifter.

Dingo

Dingoes often hunt in packs so they represent teamwork, leadership, hunting, cunning, and wit, working smart not hard. The dingo does not bark but only howls. They are generally silent, showing us the virtue of holding our tongues when we may want to comment too quickly, leading by example not by explanation, 'Do as I do, not as I say.'

Emu

Emus have a striking glare and a controlled and threatening step. They are curious, but not timid. They represent confidence, persuasion, study, focus, discernment, judgment and willpower; the nomad, travelling their journey with confidence and focus on their goals.

Possum

A nocturnal animal, they carefully move through the trees. They are a symbol of caution and the mysteries of the night. Carrying their young clinging tightly to their backs, they symbolize nurturance, agility, holding on, safety and parenting.

Cockatoo

White and yellow: Their flashing white and yellow feathers symbolize the rays of the sun, beams of inspiration and life. But their harsh calls remind us that the sun and its strength also bring fire and destruction.

Black and red: They also remind us of the fires symbolizing the red flames and the charred remains. Cleansing and renewing. Both birds are a symbol of the fire season and the power of the sun.

Magpie

Magpies are fiercely territorial when protecting their nests. However, they can also be very friendly to humans once they develop a familiarity. They do not travel far, tending to stay in a localized area and mate for life. They represent local identities, loyalty, familial bonds, protection, warriors, the home, true love, dedication and friendship.

As you learn about the animals in your area, take notes in your nature diary about the experience. Note the animal, where you saw it, anything that you notice of significance from your field guide, your own interpretation of the animal's meaning and at what time of year you saw it. In learning more about the animals of our area and their symbolic meaning, the seasons also become more meaningful. Different animals may be seen at different times of year as they migrate or move for water, food, mating, nesting or looking after their young. These movements can mark different times of year for us and bring deeper meaning to our local wheel of the year. Learning these symbols also brings the landscape alive for us as we move through it, making each encounter a message from the spirits.

Oracle Walking

Many people are familiar with working with animal spirits in dreams, meditations or astral projection work. You might have one already, perhaps even a local native animal that you have developed a connection to. The energy these animals bring to our lives can guide us and can help us understand our own nature. Working with animal energy in the inner realms is a wonderful journey. However, another way we can work with animal symbolism is through a practice called oracle walking.

To do this, simply set out for a walk or some time in nature, either with a question in mind or an open mind for receiving guidance. Then watch. See which animals come into your path. What are they doing? How are they behaving? Does it feel like a sign meant for you? Either meditate on the meaning right there and then to see if their behavior speaks to you directly, or take a note and look up the animal meaning later in a reference book or work out the meaning by looking at an animal field guide. Journal your experience to see if your insights work out to be true. You may find patterns in the appearance of certain animals, or find that one animal seems to always find you. Finding out your own is a powerful part of the path of Australian Druidry.

Tree and Plant Symbolism

As with animals, trees and plants are an important part of the modern Druid tradition and lacking relevant information relating to Australia we need to do a fair bit of the groundwork ourselves. There are some very good resources available when it comes to the symbolic meaning of Australian wildflowers such as Ian White's *Australian Bush Flower Essences* books, and Cheralyn Darcey's *Australian Wildflower Reading Cards*. When it comes to trees, however, we often need to work with our local trees ourselves. Again a good field guide for your local area can be very useful, as can the wealth of information available online. But, as with the animals, it is often of great value to make the observations directly using field guides and our own intuition.

There is a huge variety of trees and different types of forest over Australia. We have often discussed in the Druids Down Under Facebook group what we think are the most important trees and have found that even small distances can make a huge difference as to what we think should be in the list. As with the seasons, I strongly suggest you take the time to get to know the trees in your area and one way you might like to do this is by creating your own ogham (say, 'OH-am') set, as I explain in the next section.

The best way to learn more about the magical meanings of trees is to see them in nature and spend time with them ourselves, learning to feel their unique energies. We can learn much by working on our intuition and learning how to interpret their symbols through studying field guides and direct obser-vation, and also by considering the feelings we have when we are around them. Here are some examples of my own findings with trees in my local area.

Old Man Banksia – *Banksia serrata*

Banksia trees have gnarled bark and branches that look like the skin of the old and wise. The floral columns have a masculine energy, and as they turn to seed pods and open, they look like laughing mouths. As the name suggests, they symbolize men's wisdom, but also communication with spirit guides, fertility, life giving, longevity, wisdom of age, joy and laughter. They have leaves with pointy serrated edges, which symbolize the cutting wit and direct criticism that can come with the wisdom of years.

Coastal Banksia – *Banksia integrifolia*

Like a softer, more feminine version of the heath banksia. They have smooth edged leaves, smaller seed pods and always grow near the sea. They hold elder wisdom, but of a more feminine kind. Women's wisdom. Salt water wisdom. Still joyful and witty.

Bottlebrush – *Callistemon*

Bright red floral brushes, the color of our life-blood, the color of passion and love, blooming after rain and at the start of the warmer weather, they represent fertility and love. Their bottle-brush name invokes banishing, cleansing and renewing energies. Red, the color of fire, they represent death and rebirth, doorways and entrance to the underworld.

Gum Trees – *Eucalyptus*

Eucalypts represent the king of the forest, leadership, clarity, goals, focus and healing. There are hundreds of species, each with their own energies. Generally they increase energy and boost the immune system, healing and cleansing the body and providing rejuvenation and connection.

Scribbly Gum – *Eucalyptus haemastoma*

A particularly interesting eucalypt for the scribbly patterns found on the white trunks. Best seen before Barkfall, they represent study, communication, divination, mediumship and channeling. Look at the bark to find symbols and messages, paying attention to the direction they face and the elemental correspondences this represents. Or, take a piece at Barkfall, write your own message on it and leave it for the spirits.

Sydney Red Gum – *Angophora costata*
These large trees are red after losing their bark through the summertime, and gradually turn a mottled red and blue into the wintertime. They represent the change between the light and dark halves of the year. The fire energy of summer as red and the dark depths of winter as represented by blue. They also bleed a blood-colored sap, so they represent the sacred wound, warriors, grief and loss, but also healing and women's mysteries.

Iron Bark – *Eucalyptus paniculata*
A eucalypt with thick strong fibrous bark that is notoriously hard to cut. They represent strength, determination, protection, and prosperity. They also burn long and hot on the fire, and so represent longevity, endurance, passion and intensity.

Grevillea – *Grevillea*
With their long leaves and curling flowers, they represent beauty, femininity, love, peace, elegance, and grace. They can be found in many colors with white for the moon, yellow for the sun and red for fire, love and passion. Flowering about three weeks after rain, they are a symbol of fertility and growth.

Paperbark – *Melaleuca quinquenervia*
Paperbark bark is waterproof and was used by the Aboriginal people to make shelters, bowls and other items. The leaves were used to make tea by the early settlers, and the essential oil is used today for many medicinal purposes. They symbolize protection, healing, safety and security. This tree is also important for

children, art, and learning as the papery bark represents books, study and creativity.

She Oak – *Casuarina*

These beautiful trees are almost always found by water. Their long thin needles are like hair and have a gentle, feminine quality to them. They are sacred to mermaids, oceanic wisdom, rivers, lakes, tides, fishing, sea creatures, femininity, and therefore also the moon and the mother as the waters. Aboriginal people say that the whistling of the wind in their fronds is the voices of the ancestors and spirits around us.

Golden Wattle – *Acacia longifolia*

Flowering from the winter solstice to the spring equinox, these trees are sacred to the return of the sun and the warming of the year. The golden ray-like flowers represent not only the sun, but also wealth, success, good fortune, masculine energy, Awen, and abundance.

Moreton Bay Fig – *Ficus macrophylla*

These huge majestic trees have a welcoming energy that draws us in to explore them. They seem like readymade treehouses and their wide trunks create cozy sitting spots where one can feel enveloped in their comforting energy. A wonderful tree for taking time out to relax with, they symbolize protection and nurturance, comfort, playfulness and exploration. Their energy is motherly and nurturing, kind and calming. They connect us with the energy of the Earth as mother to us all.

Mangrove – *Avicennia marina*

Mangroves stand on the shore between the worlds of the land and the sea. They represent the liminal, doorways, and entrances to the otherworld, as well as balance, change, and adaptability. They work with both the energies of land and sea, but also sky, making them a plant sacred to the elements as a set of three. Being aware of two ways of being, they give us the power to embrace spiritual sight and intuition. They can be used to represent the mysteries of existence, magic and inspiration.

Making an Ogham Set

Ogham is the name of the Celtic tree alphabet. Each symbol relates to a particular type of tree and its symbolic meaning. We don't know whether the letters were originally assigned to trees in this way. This is thought to have been a later development by those studying the script in the medieval period. Nevertheless, the use of ogham letters and their association with trees and their symbols is a popular practice in modern Druidry.

Australian Druids have engaged with this idea a fair amount and there are many blogs and articles to be found on this subject online relating to different areas of the country and different theories of how we can use this system in Australia. I feel that each tree has its own unique energy and message to give and that we should spend time with those trees and observe their natures to understand what energy they represent for us, in a similar way to working with animal symbolism. I also feel we should create new ogham-like symbols to represent these trees in addition to the traditional ogham. Others have suggested that the Ogham alphabet is a complete system of spiritual energy and that the preferable way to create a set of Australian Ogham is to find trees with energies as closely equivalent as possible to the energies in the traditional alphabet. Sometimes this means having a tree aligned with two or more of the traditional ogham. In this way each of the traditional ogham has a counterpart to be found in your local area and the complete system is represented. You might be drawn to one or the other method, or perhaps interested in exploring both systems. The journey in understanding the wealth of knowledge our trees have to offer us will help you to decide.

If this is an area you are interested in exploring, an excellent way to begin is to create your own set of ogham sticks that represent the trees in your local area. The first thing to do is to find a tree you feel drawn to and which you would like to understand better. Spend some time looking at it, sitting with it, touching it, feeling its energy. Move into its space slowly and feel any change you experience in moving into it, letting it know who you are and what you would like to know. Then spend some time meditating near the tree. To do this you might like to imagine yourself as the tree, learning to feel and be as it does, or simply sit quietly, noticing any changes in your mood or the direction your thoughts lead in its presence. You might like to visit the tree on a number of occasions to become acquainted, or you may already have a familiarity with it. Once you have come to understand something about the tree and its energy it is time to ask for a stick to make your ogham with.

To do this, first find a suitable branch with a twig about 1cm in diameter and about 10cm long. Hold it as you ask the tree for its permission to take the twig for your divination purposes. You should get either a good feeling or a feeling that the tree needs the branch and that you should find another one. Take heed of your intuition here as the tree may be putting energy into new growth and taking a part of its branch may threaten its life. You will usually find that if the tree wants you to have the twig it will break surprisingly easily, but if it needs it, you will have a lot of difficulty removing it. Remember that a branch given freely will give you much more of its essence and power freely in the future.

Once you have your twig, cut it to the appropriate size and carve a section flat at one end to draw on the symbol of the tree (make one up if you like) or write its name. You could also have a symbol on one side and on the other side carve it again to write the name of the tree so you don't forget where it came from.

Remember to record what you learned about the nature of the tree in your nature diary and its meanings so that later, when you have a few sticks, you can use them for divination. Keep them in a special bag or box together. When you need to ask a question, shake the bag or box, concentrating on the question, then take a stick and read the divinatory meaning for your answer. You may be in need of the energy that tree brought to you when you were meditating with it.

Fire in the Head

Picking up her bag, she took out her drum. It was the largest thing in the bag and had made it hard to pack that morning…. That morning…wow. That seemed a world away. She had left early to get the train out to the ferry that would take her to the start of the track. On the way she had seen all kinds of people, some rushing with their heads down, some hiding their heads in their phones, many visibly suffering from the heat of the day. She didn't know any of them, but really, any one of them could have been as close to her as any of her best friends if life had taken a few different turns. She wondered how many of them spent time in the bush. She wondered how many people here had even noticed the season. It seemed the whole world was oblivious to the fact that it was summer. Every shop in the train station had been decorated with fake snow, reindeer and Santas in winter wonderlands. Men in wafer-thin red velvet Santa suits and fake beards stood outside shops selling discount swimsuits and hand fans. Songs played from shop to shop with lyrics about white Christmases, sleigh bells and snow. Surely some of these people felt all this was a bit mad too? Maybe it was time for a new song.

She breathed in and chanted Awen three times strongly, envisioning the poetic inspiration coming into her and then, she began to drum. Slow at first, like a heartbeat, then adding in secondary beats and waves of sound to bring the rhythm into greater fullness. Heartbeats, waves, rhythms… She understood now, and she began to move with the flow of it, remembering everything she had learned, and knowing she had nothing to fear in this sacred place. She wasn't alone. The spirits were with her and they were supporting her and guiding her. As she drummed, the beats started to sing to her of a song, and she began to hum along with it. One note led into another, the song of the drum itself guiding the way, and soon a melody formed. Her drumming became more intense, as her song did too, and as she sang words began to form in her mind.... Then she sang them:

Look to the land
This world is alive
The bush land is speaking
For you and for me
Let's walk this way
And look to the hillsides
The bush land is waiting
For you and for me

She sang it over and over again, letting its energy wash over her, and sending out the energy of the song as a wish for everyone to see the magic that she had seen here. She gradually let the drumming subside and, in the silence that followed, spoke her poem again.

Part 3: Practicing Australian Druidry

In Part 3 I will share with you some theory and practice on the parts that come together to make an Australian Druidry ritual and how to put it all together. I will show you an outline for ritual that you can use to shape your own and create seasonal celebrations for your area of the world and then go into the detail of the background theory of each part.

This ritual plan can be done either alone or with a group. I have laid out an outline that is suitable for a group of about six to ten people. Adjustments would need to be made for other groups, but the general plan would be the same. The 'seasonal celebration' part of the ritual is up to you. This is where you will look to your nature diary, consider the symbolism of the time, and create an activity for you and your group that will help you all to come into alignment with it. This might take the form of a time to meditate, a time to share feelings and wishes on a certain theme, creating an offering, planting a seed, dancing, etc. Looking to books about ritual will help you to get an idea of what is possible, but do what feels right and what feels like a coming into alignment with the energy of nature around you.

Before you begin your ritual there are a few things to consider. First you will need to find a suitable and special place to hold your ritual. This might be in nature, a garden, in the home in the colder months, or any other place you feel drawn to, though I would recommend ritual spaces in nature whenever possible as the main purpose of the ritual is to connect with nature and the seasonal cycles. Next you will want to set up an altar, or focal point in the centre. Lay down a colored piece of cloth and on that add decorations of seasonal flowers, or other items which mark the time of year and your ritual purpose. You can also add symbols of the elements (see 5. Land, Sea and Sky). Make the space beautiful and tidy and comfortable for yourself and the people in your circle. You might like to energetically cleanse the space with incense, perhaps using a loose blend of native aromatic leaves and charcoal, or stick incense, or a sage smudging stick. You can also energetically cleanse each circle member before the ritual by gently wafting the smoke around them with a feather or a leafy branch.

To begin, gather together standing in a circle around the altar decorations. Be silent for a few moments and take time to allow any conversation or other thoughts about your day to subside, and then begin. The following chapters will give you more detail on each section, but all together the ritual plan will be as follows:

1. Connecting with the spirits of place
2. The round of Amergín
3. The call for peace
4. Welcome to the three ancestors
5. Land, sea and sky
6. Seasonal celebration
7. Awen
8. Eisteddfod
9. Feast
10. Closing

Note: You may find that you do not wish to use these ritual elements in the order I explain them, or you may have personal preferences as to how things should be done in regards to circle casting or recognizing the elements. This is fine. Use what works for you, and set aside what does not. It should be noted that circle practice in Druidry is quite different to some other magical practices such as in witchcraft. In Wicca and witchcraft the object of creating a circle is to hold power within and guard from external negative influences. In Druidry, however, this is not the case. Instead, this is a practice of coming into presence with what always is, and recognizing the sacredness of the present moment.

It is a communion with nature, the ancestors, and the spirits, and a time for opening ourselves to creative expression. Also the action of magic here is not so much in expressing our will for change in the world, but rather through aligning ourselves with the flow of the season and the world around us, our lives become more magical as a result. The power of our creative expression is our magic, and it is through our connection with nature that we find that creativity.

1. Connecting with the Spirits of Place

Connecting with the spirits of place is something we do at the beginning of our circles. It is a time to be quiet and listen to the place we are in. To learn to hear first, rather than to speak first, is important. So easily our conversation with the land can become one-sided. Before our circle even begins, we often take a little time to explore around the area, perhaps looking for a special stone, a feather or a leaf we could add to the altar space.

When we are ready to begin the circle, we stand together with our hands joined and simply listen to the energies of the space. We notice animals we see and hear, we listen for the wind, we feel the touch of the sun and the breeze, and we smell the earthy scents around us. We also sense ancestral presences and other spirits who may reside in the place we are in. This practice is grounding, centering, and helps us to recognize the sacredness of our immediate environment, and connect with it.

2. The Round of Amergín

The part of the ritual we call 'The Round of Amergín'. It has an historical background as the practice is based on a poem from the *Lebor Gabála Érenn* (The Book of the Taking of Ireland), called The Song of Amergín. The book describes the six waves of 'invasions' or settlements of different races of beings in Ireland: the people of Cessair, the people of Partholón, the people of Nemed, the Fir Bolg, the Tuatha Dé Danann, and the Milesians. The first four races were wiped out or forced to leave the land and often represent the wild forces of nature in the mythology. The fifth group, the Tuatha Dé Danann, were the deities and magical beings who are associated with burial mounds and the other-world. The sixth group, the Milesians, were the race of human beings, specifically the Gaelic people who came from the area now known as Spain. Amergín was the chief poet of the Milesians, or 'the Sons of Míl'. In the story of their arrival in Ireland, Amergín speaks this poem with his first step onto the land, in so doing, shows his connection with the land and the people's belonging there. The poem reads:

I am the wind upon the sea
I am a wave upon the ocean
I am the murmur of billows
I am an ox of seven fights
I am an eagle upon a rock
I am a ray of the sun
I am the fairest of plants
I am a wild board in valor
I am a salmon in a pool
I am a lake upon a plain
I am a word of cunning art
I am the point of a spear in battle

I am the God that puts fire in the head
Who brings light to the gathering on the hilltop?
Who announces the ages of the moon?
Who knows the place where the sun has its rest?
Who finds springs of clear water?
Who calls the fishes from the ocean's depths?
Who causes them to come to shore?
Who changes the shape of headland and hill?
A bard whom seafarers call upon to prophesy
Spears shall be wielded
I prophesy victory
And all good things
And so ends my song[1]

Amergín was connecting with the land of Ireland, becoming it, and the words he uses evoke elements of the land that would have been familiar to anyone who lived there at that time, and many who still do today. When I was in the UK attending the circle at Avebury, the Round of Amergín was a technique used to connect the circle with the energy of the land and the season. Rather than reciting the words of the original poem, instead we invoked parts of the landscape around us and what we felt connected to in the moment and in our environment, always using the words 'I am' to begin our invocation. Each person would have a turn and if the group was small, perhaps we would speak multiple times until we felt that the space had been acknowledged sufficiently.

In bringing what I had learned in the UK home to Australia I found that this was a very useful part of making our rituals feel at home in the spaces we performed them and connecting us with nature. We most often held our rituals in the bush so connecting with that landscape was really special, but the technique can also be used in gardens or indoors with different effects, making each space feel sacred. When we are in the bush our invocations often sound like:

I am the whisper of she oak needles
I am the white cockatoos that fly overhead
I am the bream which jumps in the lake
I am the laughing kookaburra...

When we are in gardens our invocations might include a combination of native and introduced species from all over the world, and honoring their presence too can be a very special element of the ritual. After all the purpose of this is not to make native species seem 'better', but to include them in the whole of our appreciation of nature. An indoor ritual may invoke the strength and protection of the home, the wind howling outside, the rain tapping on the windows, the glow of the candle on the altar. This is a time to explore what feels good and connect more deeply with the spirits of place.

3. The Call for Peace

We all face the east. The ritual leader raises their hands and says, 'May there be peace in the east,' sending out love and peace to all beings to the east of us in the world. All reply to this by repeating the words, 'May there be peace in the east.' The ritual leader then moves to the north, west and south and this is repeated in those directions. The ritual leader then circles the group one more time saying, 'May there be peace in this world, the underworld and the otherworld. May there be peace.' All say in reply, 'May there be peace.'

This practice positions the circle in regards to the rest of the world by acknowledging the four directions and three worlds. It is also a gesture of peace, love and compassion for all. We do not call in the elements at the quarters. I explain why in 5. Land, Sea and Sky.

4. Welcome to the Three Ancestors

Honoring ancestors is another very important part of the Druid tradition. Many of the old Celtic myths involve long lines of family lineages and the belief in reincarnation showed a sense of the dead being forever with us in different forms. Also, many of what we might call 'Gods' of the Celtic tradition could be considered ancestors, as they were more often than not seen as heroes with superhuman abilities or otherworldly connections rather than immortal abstract influences on the human realm. Even the *Lebor Gabála Érenn* speaks of the Tuatha Dé Danann as an earlier race of Ireland, rather than metaphysical beings. Ancestors are those who now dwell in the spirit realm. In the circles I run we have explored the idea of there being three kinds of ancestors. We generally refer to them as:

- The ancestors of our bloodlines
- The ancestors of our inspirations and
- The ancestors of the land

The ancestors of our bloodlines represent the family tree of our past and the many stories of people and places that led to our being alive in this moment. When we come together as a group to practice, we recognize and honor the many paths of people who led to us as individuals, no matter where we have come from. It is a beautiful way of coming together in our diversity. We honor and give gratitude for those who have given us this body to exist in, and recognize the stories we inherit with that lineage. Indeed, we have had people of many different backgrounds come together in our circles and this practice helps everyone to feel welcome, and brought together by the land and our shared inspiration in Druidry. As Australia is a multicultural country this has made our path feel less exclusive and more welcoming.

Many people find that exploring their family tree gives them a great sense of their own personal identity. Learning about the routes of migrations and languages over time and the cultures of our ancestors can tell us a lot about ourselves. Many people find this information easily. Often a family member has already created a family tree, or there is easy access to records online. However, some people are adopted, and find this information much more difficult to access. In the cases of a few of our adopted circle members, they have chosen to find out the origins of their bloodline ancestors by taking a DNA test. You can find these online and the detail they give on the movement of your ancestors over many centuries can help you to understand the stories that you hold within you, and send your gratitude to your ancestors of bloodline.

This brings us to the ancestors of our inspiration. These are our teachers and guides – those who have inspired us and helped shape our minds. These include the teachers of our tradition in Druidry both modern and ancient as well as teachings each of us have been inspired by as individuals. Each of us, through our lives, has gained wisdom and insight through our spirituality, and also through teachers and guides who have helped us see truth in many ways, helping us to become the people we are today. These could be spiritual leaders of other traditions, authors, poets, philosophers, parents, friends, role models, etc. We recognize all pathways to wisdom, and all knowledge that has led us to be the individuals we are today. For each person the additions to the path of Druidry will be a bit different. Honoring all of the ancestors of our inspirations is a way of recognizing that we are all unique and have different interests, but that we are brought together in our sharing of the ritual inspired by Druidry. This is also a way of making members of our circle feel welcome, even if they have different opinions to us, we can all celebrate together and recognize our differences as well as our similarities.

If relevant to our ritual, it is in this section that we would also welcome the energy of any deities we wish to work with. Some Australian Druids find working with northern hemisphere deities in the Australian landscape feels strange, preferring to work directly with nature energies instead. It can feel as though we are dragging them away from the land where they belong. However, some feel that particular deities are more easily called than others because of their associations also being present here. For example, Brigid, being a Goddess of the home and hearth, crafts, and poetry, feels more easily called, while deities whose stories relate to specific locations or natural formations of the lands they came from may be more difficult to connect with. There are, however, many deities whose presence we can feel in the land here, and exploring which of their stories might be relevant to our new seasonal celebrations is another area for our exploration.

The ancestors of the land are the next group of ancestors we welcome. They are those who have gone before us in the land we are in. Whether we think of 'the land' as a specific location, a town, area, or country, it is the human stories there that we recognize as being integral to our being there. In our local area this means recognizing and voicing acknowledgement to our local indigenous community and their elders past and present, it means recognizing the history of the pioneers who settled there, and the many human stories that led to the place where we hold our rituals being available to us. Acknowledging the ancestors of the land means that no matter where we are, we should honor that place, its history; its spirits.

First of all it is a good idea to find out the name of the traditional owners of the place you are holding your ritual. This can be done quite easily with an online search. Acknowledging traditional owners and their elders both past and present, is a good addition to this section of your ritual, and a way of showing respect to Indigenous people that they have specifically asked for. Knowing a little about the history of the place you are in, from their perspective, can also be good. Were there battles? What happened in regards to the stolen generations? Is there hurt and pain in the spirit realms as a result of this that needs to be addressed? Simply recognizing the history and well-wishing the departed at this point can bring positive energy to both your circle and the spirits. Noticing any feelings you get from the land's spirits at this point can also be useful. Though you may have felt for it at the beginning, check again: are you welcome to do your ritual here, or are they warning you of something, or even asking you to leave? I have found in some places I have been asked to move my ritual space to another area and begin again. This hasn't happened often, but it is important to be sensitive to the intuitions we feel in regards to the spirits around us. If we learn to listen to them, they will also show us the most wonderful places too. I've been guided to beautiful carving sites and special caves in my area many times by learning to listen. Respect and honor the spirits of the land and they will look after you.

The history of the space you are in since European settlement can also be good to know, as Indigenous histories are only a part of the history of many areas. There are a few things to consider.

- Are you in a garden, reserve, state forest or national park?
- What was the history of its protection and care?
- Have there been protests to save it?
- Was it gifted to the community by a former landowner?
- Have there been battles with developers to keep it as a natural space?
- Has it always been a park? If not, what else is it used for, and by whom?

All these questions help us to understand the ancestors of the land who are the many people who have lived to help make the space we are in available to us at the time of our ritual. They have shaped its history and energy. Whether we know this story or not, we can send our welcome to those spirits and express gratitude for their efforts. The more we know about a place, the greater our connection with the ancestors of the land becomes.

When welcoming the three ancestors into your ritual space you could use a simple invocation similar to the following. You can also make it much longer to include information discussed above as you gain more knowledge, but this is a good place to start.

We welcome the ancestors of our bloodlines,
Those who have gone before us
Whose spirits dwell within us
Without whom we would not be

We welcome the ancestors of our inspiration
Our traditions, our muses, our Awen
Whose spirits have guided us here
And made us who we are today

We welcome the ancestors of the land
We acknowledge the (Indigenous) people, and elders past and
    present
And the spirits of all those who have been here before us
Who hold the stories of this place

We welcome you and ask for your blessings in this rite

Honoring Indigenous Wisdom

Aboriginal and Torres Strait Islander people have been incredibly generous in sharing many of their stories about the Australian land and its plants and animals, as well as access to many of their sacred sites and other important places. Many of these stories and places offer us a doorway into seeing how these ancient cultures viewed and continue to view the sacred energies of the land. Honoring what we have been given access to, and learning what we can with gratitude, is an important part of connecting with the spirits of the land in the places we practice Australian Druidry. We should, however, bear in mind the sensitive issues around appropriation and taking what has not been given freely. Remembering to be respectful of the traditions, learning as much as we can about cultural sensitivities and other Indigenous issues, and always making sure we have permission to pass along knowledge.

Showing our respect might be as simple as being sure to find out where a story comes from before we tell it to others, or including a welcome to country in our rituals. Respecting traditions of secrecy is also very important, particularly if we have been told a story by an Indigenous person in confidence. They will always tell you if there are restrictions as to who can and cannot be told a story. You might like to bring a story into your circle, perhaps as a part of the eisteddfod section (see 8. Eisteddfod), or maybe you have found a local story of the land that is relevant to the season? As a guide, I have been told that it is always acceptable to share a story if it has been published, and it is considered respectful to acknowledge the traditional owners of the story before you share it.

It is also important to respect Indigenous sacred sites and their rules for engagement with them. I would generally not recommend holding rituals on Indigenous sacred sites, unless perhaps you have been invited to do so by an Indigenous person. We have often held rituals near places that are important to the Guringai people of the Northern Beaches in Sydney, but generally we visit the site and then find a place close by to do our ritual as a gesture of respect.

Lastly, the best way to learn more about Indigenous culture is face to face. Find out if there is a local centre for Indigenous culture in your area, or maybe a local elder runs talks or bushwalks you can attend. Many places have spaces for cultural activities and sharing and making friends with people is the best way you can learn more about how our spiritual traditions and relationships with the land can complement each other. As with the land, we should be sure to listen more than we speak. If we really want to learn, ask questions.

5. Land, Sea and Sky

In our rituals we call in and welcome the spirits of the three realms of land, sea and sky. In this part of our ritual we are welcoming the essences of these three realms, as both parts of the physical world and also as elements that make up the universe. This may be a new way of looking at the elements for you if you have worked with the elements before. We have found the use of three realms or elements to be useful in a number of ways. It creates a shift of thinking from the four elemental systems (earth, air, fire and water) that often create confusion for people practicing in Australia, and it also offers some new insights into the nature of the elements.

Let me elaborate. In many Pagan rituals and northern hemisphere explanations of Druidry and other Pagan traditions you will find the elements as a group of four: earth, air, fire and water. They are generally associated with the directions of north, east, south and west respectively. In Australia, as with the seasonal wheel, people tend to make some adjustments. Often they will switch north and south to make more sense of our position in the southern hemisphere so that south becomes earth, east remains air, north becomes fire and west remains water. Others, particularly those living on the eastern coast of Australia, have worked with an idea has come to be known as 'Sydney Standard Quarter Calling', where south becomes air, in relation to the wild southerly winds, east becomes water in reference to the whopping great Pacific Ocean right there in front of us, fire is north for the hotter areas of the country and the swing of the sun's arc, and west is earth relating to the bulk of the land we live on and the mountains.

In circles I have attended over the years I've found people using all three systems, and each time there is good reason for doing so. Some maintain that the elements are in the same directions no matter where we are in the world, and so use the traditional system, many do the north-south switch, and in Sydney it is very popular to use the 'Sydney Standard', but certainly not a rule. What I have found, however, is that having these many systems and different people being comfortable with different ones, is that when we come together as a group, we get confused; we forget which system we are using; we stumble over our words or say the wrong element in the wrong direction. To avoid this feeling of hesitancy which seems to create a block for the flow of the ritual, we decided to omit this part altogether and invoke the elements along with the realms of land, sea and sky, and Awen instead. We face the centre only when welcoming them, and feel that the cardinal points are recognized sufficiently in the call for peace.

The three realms of land, sea and sky relate to a slightly different elemental system. Land is similar to the earth element and also includes principle of 'calas' (say CAH-lass), sea is similar to water and includes the principle of 'gwyar' (say GOO-yar), and sky is like a combination of air and fire and includes the principle of 'nwyfre'. This three-principle system of elements works slightly differently to the four element system, and considering both can be a way of expanding our understanding of the elements as not simply separate entities, but also part of a flowing whole which can be separated infinitely or brought together into unity. The principle relating to land is calas. It is the stable, solid, physical part of our existence, the 'stuff' we are made of. Within our bodies it is our bone, teeth and muscle. Gwyar is process, action, time, movement, growth and decay, as well as liquid substances. It literally means 'blood', but refers also to water and fluidity. Within our bodies it is our blood, tears, sweat and reproductive fluids. Nwyfre is the metaphysical; that which exists without form. It is the life force, the soul, the spirit, the spark of life and also thought, ideas, magic and wit. Within our bodies it is our breath, our heat, our thoughts and our spirit.

John Michael Greer gives a great explanation of the relationship of the elements as a group of three in a contemplation of your dinner:

The calas element of your dinner is the raw material: meat, grains, vegetables and fruit. The gwyar element is the cooking process that turns the raw material into the meal on your plate. The nwyfre element is the mental dimension: the selection of ingredients, the choice of recipes, and the skill and personality of the cook.[2]

You might like to call the quarters as earth, air, fire and water; assigning them to the directions in one of the traditional ways, and also call in the spirits of land, sea and sky as a separate consideration. Another possibility, which we have used from time to time, is to call land, sea and sky as relating to earth, water and air, and then bring in the fire element with the chant of Awen, as Awen can be understood as 'the fire in the head'. You can see an example of this in the story of the cave ritual in this book. What feels right to you, and brings you a greater feeling of connection and flow, is the right path to take – this is yet another area of Australian Druidry, and Australian Paganism more generally, that people are still discovering for themselves.

Land

Welcoming the spirits of the realm of land is different to welcoming the ancestors of the land. The ancestors of the land discussed in the last chapter refers specifically to human spirit presences and histories, while in this section we focus more on the plants and animals associated to the realm of the land and the elements of earth and calas. We envision the forest, the trees, shrubs, bushes and grass, and all the animals that live there, as well as the land's form and shape. It is good to consider which animals live in the area, particularly mammals and reptiles. Have you heard wallabies jumping through the bushes, or seen a possum there at night? Are there lizards or snakes around, or echidnas, emus, koalas or wombats or any others? We feel into their presence and welcome their energy into our circle. It is also a good idea to find out about the lay of the land in your area. Where are there pockets of nature? Are there any significant landforms like mountains, large rocks, valleys, or different kinds of ecosystems? Looking at maps and satellite images online can be helpful, but better yet, head out for some bushwalking before your ritual and get to know your land first hand. An example of what might be said during ritual to welcome the spirits of land is:

We call on the spirits of the land; spirits of the ground beneath our feet, of the grass, the trees, the animals of the bush, the gravity and mass of the planet we call our home. We welcome the energy of Calas that is our bones, teeth, nails, hair and muscle and the matter that makes up all of existence. We ask that you bring into our circle solidity, groundedness, stability and truth. Hail and welcome.
(All repeat, 'Hail and welcome.')

Sea

Welcoming the spirits of the realm of sea, we focus on the oceans, seas, and other waterways, the rains, the plants and animals that make that realm their home, and the element of water and gwyar. We envision the waves of the ocean, undersea gardens, coral reefs, lake bottoms, riverways, fish, crustaceans and aquatic plants. We consider any waterways close by and what kinds of creatures we might find there. There might be fish jumping in a lake nearby, or yabbies between the rocks of a creek, or perhaps a platypus, frog or turtle. We feel into their presence and welcome their energy into our circle. In learning about your area you might also consider finding out where your tap water comes from, where there are local dams and what they are used for. Trace the paths of creeks and riverways, notice where there are floodplains or wetlands and how these change through the year. Be aware of tidal changes in the ocean if you live by the sea, as well as swell movements and the effects they have on water quality or the presence of fish species, whales and dolphins.

An example of what might be said during ritual to welcome the spirits of sea is:

We call on the spirits of the sea and all waterways; spirits of the great oceans, the streams, the rivers and the lakes, of our own tears and blood, of all the fish and other creatures of the sea, and the waters of life. We welcome the energy of gwyar that is the force of change, movement, action, growth and decay. We ask that they bring us the power to create change, to feel the moment and to come into presence. Hail and welcome.

(All repeat, 'Hail and welcome.')

Sky

Welcoming the spirits of the realm of sky we consider all winged creatures, the weather, the sun, moon and stars, and our place in the vast universe. We also consider the elements air, fire and nwyfre. We envision the sky in all its forms – day, night, sunny, filled with stars, bright clear blue, overcast and grey, or filled with fluffy clouds – as well as the sun, moon and stars. We consider any flying creatures we have seen nearby whether birds or insects. Can we see them or hear them? Finding out about the movement of bird species can help us to see markers through the year, and recognizing their presence in the land is a part of this section of the ritual. We notice when they are mating and nesting, when they are noisy and feeding in groups, or when they are out and about with new young.

The presence of insects is quite prominent in the summer, while not so much in the winter. We will notice the first call of the cicadas, or the arrival of mosquitoes or flies. We need not feel that by calling them into our circle we are encouraging more of them to come bother us. Rather this is a point where we respect their presence as a part of the ecosystem and the web of life. Also take some time to consider the movement of the wind through the year, the different weather patterns, or times of the year when certain constellations can be seen at night. We feel into all of this and welcome the energy into our circle. An example of what might be said during ritual to call in the spirits of sky is:

We call on the spirits of the sky; spirits of the wind and the air, of the birds, the weather, the sun, stars and moon, of the clouds, of our thoughts and consciousness and all spirit. We welcome the spark of life that animates all being. And we ask that they bring us clear thought, intelligence and wisdom. Hail and welcome.
(All repeat, 'Hail and welcome.')

6. Seasonal Celebration

In this part of the ritual you can look to the information in Part 1 about the wheel of the year, and to your own nature diary to find ideas about what you can do to celebrate the season. I would encourage you to begin this section with a chance for people to share their experiences of the season. What have they noticed changing lately and how have they been feeling? What has been happening in the world and how has that been affecting people? What is the general mood and what is needed to bring things into balance?

There are many possibilities for how you might celebrate this, and over time you will develop more ideas about what will work well. Don't be afraid to try new ideas and be a little experimental. What is most important is that the action feels meaningful. Some things we have done that have worked well include making a floating raft to bring a blessing to the ocean and water ways at Wind Change Festival out of natural items. We gave our blessings to the raft and then sent it out into the lake. At Flower Festival one year we asked for inspiration while lighting many tea light candles on the altar. Another time at Fire Festival we had a ritual shower in a natural waterfall as a rebirthing. At Moon Festival one time we took turns at giving each other oracle card readings.

The best thing to do is consider the meaning of the time of year, consider what it is you feel you need, and add something of this into your ritual for alignment with the season. This is where the magic happens. It is in aligning with nature and becoming a part of the flow of life around us, that we begin to open ourselves up to our creative expression; our Awen.

7. Awen

'Awen' means 'flowing inspiration' and is the creative spirit that flows through us when we perform or create our art. It is the 'fire in the head' spoken of in the Song of Amergín. It is to be inspired; to have spirit within us, guiding the flow of our actions. When the Awen flows, our actions become our art. Each of us has an art, and it can come in many forms, though in ritual we work to bring it forth in us through playing music, singing, and sharing poetry and stories. Learning to perform with flow and confidence is a method of touching spirit and touching truth. This is incredibly important to the Bard, but also has importance for the Ovate and Druid paths too. In Australian Druidry many people are working towards creating new poetry, songs and stories about this land and its energies and messages. We are slowly creating a wealth of new inspired myths and legends that speak of the energy of this sacred landscape. Awen is used as a chant that helps us to be spontaneously creative and have the inspiration for poetic performance. To call it we begin by holding hands in a circle. Then, after taking a deep breath, we intone the word 'Awen' as (AH-OO-EH-NN) over a full outbreath. We do this three times. This is done before Bardic performances or eisteddfod.

The story of Taliesin is integral to the learning of many Bards, and is the keystone myth of OBOD's courses. It is through tasting the three drops of Awen, and then a journey of exploring the elements through shapeshifting into various animals with the Goddess Cerridwen, that the boy Gwion Bach is transformed into Taliesin, the Greatest Bard of Britain. The connection with the land and its animals has an important role to play in the gaining of inspiration, as we can also see in the Song of Amergín discussed earlier. Our entire practice leads us towards inspiration. It is through our connection to the land that we find our art and, with that, the gift we have for the world and our purpose in this life.

When we express our gifts, talents and arts with the flow of Awen, we are moving into being a part of spirit becoming manifest in the world as truth, beauty, and wisdom.

8. Eisteddfod

During ritual, the eisteddfod (say eye-STETH-fod) is a time for sharing our stories, songs and poetry inspired by the season. Some groups will be naturally musical, enjoying a jam and creating music on the spot, while others tell wild and fascinating stories and share inspired poems. Others find these arts more challenging and for them this can be a time to give their expression a go, learning to get the Awen to flow. Learning both to write the poems and to memorize and perform them are skills that help us to experience the flow of Awen in us. To fully experience it, we need a combination of dedicated practice, and also surrendering to the flow of spirit. A great book to help with your bardic learning is *The Bardic Handbook* by Kevan Manwarring. It gives a lot of tips and ideas for increasing your bardic skills.

In our circle, over time we have brought along poems and songs specifically for the season and take turns to share them as a performance. The following words are the lyrics of a song written by Adrienne K. Piggott of the Pagan band Spiral Dance. We met at a workshop in 2012 and though she lives in South Australia, she has seen similarities in the wheel of the year I presented and the changes in her local area. I hope that her words will help you to feel the Awen flow and inspire you to create some poetry about the place where you live.

Goddess of the Southern Land – by Adrienne K. Piggott

The spirits of this place have whispered me a song
With the north wind in the she-oak tree when the summer days are long
Through the greening of the hills when the winter rains have come
And now I know they're telling me it's to this land that I belong.

Black crow flies on silent wings across an endless blue
Magpie carols and boobook calls beneath the full spring moon
Faerie wren and his followers are dancing with the fae
And brother kookaburra wakes the sky people to bring the sun each
    day

Chorus:
    Goddess of this Southern Land I'm yet to find your name
    I've been travelling the pathways from where my ancestors came
    But now I long to hear the songlines that are singing through your
        veins
    Goddess of this Southern Land I'm yet to know your name

Rainbow serpent mother, protector of the land
In the dreaming time awoke and moved her body 'cross the sand
And shaped the land into being, making hills and mountains rise,
Filling water holes and rivers, she brought the earth to life.

The wild Mount Lofty Ranges have given me my home
A place when the earth was young, a mighty giant roamed
And journeyed through the landscape between the rivers and the
    plain
His body formed the mountain range in the place where he was
    slain

I know Brigid's walking with me when the wild flowers have come
And when the wattle flowers into life the color of the sun
In misty mountain bush land, the smell of eucalyptus after rain
And the bark fall signals that it's time to celebrate Beltane.

The magic of your dreamtime, the story of this land
There's so much of your wildness that I'm yet to understand
And I know I am a newcomer and my journey's just begun
But your ancient voice has told me that the land and I are one

8. Eisteddfod

The spirits of this place have whispered me a song
With the north wind in the she-oak tree when the summer days are
*   long*
Through the greening of the hills when the winter's rains have
*   come*
And now I know they're telling me it's to this land that I belong

9. Feast

In ritual we bring our minds into different states to our regular way of being. We feel inspired, we work with spirits and energies, we perform symbolic actions that can change us and bring insight and often emotional feelings. At the end of the ritual we have some food to bring us back again. It is also a time to give thanks for the food and drink that sustains us and all the forces and people responsible for bringing them to us.

You might like to incorporate dinner into your ritual, or you might just have a simple plate of bread or biscuits and some juice, wine, water, or any other drink. Learning about native foods or growing your own vegetables to share and incorporating them into what you eat for this part of the ritual can even make it a part of further connecting with the land. Some ideas for native food might include damper with native hibiscus jam with wattle seed coffee, or macadamia nut biscuits and lemon myrtle cordial. Collecting cherry lilli pillies in February to share can be a bright addition to the altar. Native foods are great, but you can also bringing your own home grown or home-made food. Perhaps a family recipe to honor your ancestors? It all adds to the meaning of the ritual.

We always enjoy sharing a meal together during our circles. Before eating the food and drink, we give thanks for all those who worked towards bringing them to us and to fully appreciate the energy that they give us. Also, we give thanks to the plants themselves and the powers of nature as well as the farmers and the workers who put so much effort in to make them available to us. Before eating or drinking, use your senses of smell, sight and touch to fully appreciate them. Touch them, smell them, look at their beauty. Savor every mouthful, letting it become part of you. They are the land, and through eating them, you become one with it. We also often pass the food and drink around the circle, taking a piece of food and a sip of drink with the blessings of, 'May you never hunger,' and, 'May you never thirst,' passed around the circle with them.

10. Closing

In closing the circle we again hold hands and say something along the lines of, 'We express our thanks to the spirits of land, sea and sky, the three ancestors and the spirits of place for being with us in our ritual. We bid you hail and farewell.'

We then also give thanks to each other for coming along and bringing our energy to the circle.

The Journey Forward

I hope that you have enjoyed reading this book. I hope you have learnt ways that you can celebrate the seasons and honor the ancestors that are meaningful to you and your life's journey. I hope too that you will be inspired to share your journey with others, as it is through our sharing and inspiring each other that our sacred connection with this land will grow. If you would like to be involved with the Druids Down Under group online, you can find us on Facebook where we would be glad to hear about your experiences in this journey. You can also find a lot of further information about Australian Paganism, Druidry more generally, and other information in the next section of recommended reading.

By the spirits of the ancestors, the energies of land, sea, and sky, and the inspiration of Awen, I bid you hail and farewell.

Bibliography and Recommended Reading

Australian Paganism

Barton, Murray, Juliet Marillier and Christopher Oakeley (eds), *Southern Echoes: An Anthology of Druid Writings from the Southern Hemisphere*, Insubstantial Technologies: Helena Valley, (year unknown). Available through the Druid Network online.

Ezzy, Doug, *Practicing the Witch's Craft: Real Magic Under a Southern Sky*, Allen and Unwin: Crows Nest, 2003

Modern Druidry

Billington, Penny, *The Path of Druidry: Walking the Ancient Green Way*, Llewellyn: Woodbury, 2011

Carr-Gomm, Philip (ed.), *The Druid Renaissance: The Voice of Druidry Today*, Thorsons: London, 1996

Greer, John Michael, *The Druidry Handbook: Spiritual Practice Rooted in the Living Earth*, Red Wheel: Boston, 2006

MacEowen, Frank, *The Mist Filled Path*, New World Library: Novato, 2002

Manwaring, Kevan, *The Bardic Handbook*, Gothic Image Productions: Glastonbury, 2006

Nichols, Ross, John Matthews and Philip Carr-Gomm (eds.), *The Book of Druidry*, Thorsons: London, 1975

Restall-Orr, Emma, *Principles of Druidry*, Thorsons: London, 1998

Restall-Orr, Emma, *Ritual – A Guide to Life, Love and Inspiration*, Thorsons: London, 2000

Restall-Orr, Emma, *Living with Honour: A Pagan Ethics*, O Books: Winchester; Washington, 2007

Rowan, Arthur, *The Lore of the Bard: A Guide to the Celtic and Druid Mysteries*, Llewellyn: St Paul, 2003

Shallcrass, Philip, *Druidry: A Practical and Inspirational Guide*, Piatkus: London, 2000

History of Druids

Hutton, Ronald, *Blood and Mistletoe: The History of the Druids of Britain*, Yale University Press: New Haven; London, 2009

Hutton, Ronald, *The Druids*, Hambledon Continuum: London, 2007

Celtic Mythology

Berresford Ellis, Peter, *The Mammoth Book of Celtic Myths and Legends*, Constable & Robinson: London, 1999

Gantz, Jeffery, *Early Irish Myths and Sagas*, Penguin Books: Harmondsworth, 1981

Gantz, Jeffery, *The Mabinogion*, Penguin Books: London, 1976

Plants and Animals

Darcey, Cheralyn, *Australian Wildflower Reading Cards*, Rockpool Publishing: Summer Hill, 2014

Kindred, Glennie, *The Tree Ogham*, Glennie Kindred: Nottingham, 1997

King, Scott Alexander, *Animal Dreaming Oracle Cards*, Blue Angel Gallery Australia: Glen Waverley, 2007

Menkhorst, Peter and Frank Knight, *A Field Guide to the Mammals of Australia*, (second edition), Oxford University Press: South Melbourne, 2001 (2004)

Pizzey, Graham, and Frank Knight, *The Field Guide to the Birds of Australia*, (eighth edition), Harper Collins: Sydney, 1980 (2007)

White, Ian, *Australian Bush Flower Essences*, Bantam Books (Transworld Publishers): Moorebank, Australia, 1991 (2002)

Indigenous Wisdom

Cowan, James, *Aborigine Dreaming – An Introduction to the Wisdom and Thought of the Aboriginal Traditions of Australia*, Thorsons: London, 1992 (2002)

Reed, A.W., *Aboriginal Myths – Tales of the Dreamtime*, Reed New Holland: Sydney, 1978 (2002)

Pahl, Anja-Karina, with Jacinta Tobin, *Gondwana Dreaming: Tools for Transformation*, Earth Education: Gembrook, 2001

Web Resources and Blogs

Druids Down Under on Facebook – https://www.facebook.com/groups/druidsdownunder/

Druids Down Under Blog – http://druidsdownunder.blogspot.com.au/

The British Druid Order (BDO) – http://www.druidry.co.uk/

The Order of Bards Ovates and Druids (OBOD) – http://www.druidry.org/

Ár nDraíocht Féin: A Druid Fellowship (ADF) – https://www.adf.org/

Forest Spirituality with Julie Brett podcast – http://forestspirituality.podbean.com/

Endnotes

1. This version is from Shallcrass, Philip, 'The Bardic Tradition and the Song of The Land,' in Carr-Gomm, Philip (ed.) *The Druid Renaissance: The Voice of Druidry Today*, Thorsons: London, 1996, p.55. Permission from the author to publish this met with great thanks. You can read more about Philip Shallcrass' work in Druidry at his blog 'Greywolf's Lair' at greywolf.druidry.co.uk and more about the British Druid Order at www.druidry.co.uk

2. Greer, John Michael, *The Druidry Handbook: Spiritual Practice Rooted in the Living Earth*, Red Wheel: Boston, 2006, p.61

Moon Books

PAGANISM & SHAMANISM

What is Paganism? A religion, a spirituality, an alternative belief system, nature worship? You can find support for all these definitions (and many more) in dictionaries, encyclopaedias, and text books of religion, but subscribe to any one and the truth will evade you. Above all Paganism is a creative pursuit, an encounter with reality, an exploration of meaning and an expression of the soul. Druids, Heathens, Wiccans and others, all contribute their insights and literary riches to the Pagan tradition. Moon Books invites you to begin or to deepen your own encounter, right here, right now. If you have enjoyed this book, why not tell other readers by posting a review on your preferred book site. Recent bestsellers from Moon Books are:

Journey to the Dark Goddess
How to Return to Your Soul
Jane Meredith
Discover the powerful secrets of the Dark Goddess and transform your depression, grief and pain into healing and integration.
Paperback: 978-1-84694-677-6 ebook: 978-1-78099-223-5

Shamanic Reiki
Expanded Ways of Working with Universal Life Force Energy
Llyn Roberts, Robert Levy
Shamanism and Reiki are each powerful ways of healing;
together, their power multiplies. *Shamanic Reiki* introduces
techniques to help healers and Reiki practitioners tap ancient
healing wisdom.
Paperback: 978-1-84694-037-8 ebook: 978-1-84694-650-9

Pagan Portals – The Awen Alone
Walking the Path of the Solitary Druid
Joanna van der Hoeven
An introductory guide for the solitary Druid, *The Awen Alone*
will accompany you as you explore, and seek out your own
place within the natural world.
Paperback: 978-1-78279-547-6 ebook: 978-1-78279-546-9

A Kitchen Witch's World of Magical Herbs & Plants
Rachel Patterson
A journey into the magical world of herbs and plants, filled with
magical uses, folklore, history and practical magic. By popular
writer, blogger and kitchen witch, Tansy Firedragon.
Paperback: 978-1-78279-621-3 ebook: 978-1-78279-620-6

Medicine for the Soul
The Complete Book of Shamanic Healing
Ross Heaven
All you will ever need to know about shamanic healing and
how to become your own shaman...
Paperback: 978-1-78099-419-2 ebook: 978-1-78099-420-8

Shaman Pathways – The Druid Shaman
Exploring the Celtic Otherworld
Danu Forest
A practical guide to Celtic shamanism with exercises and
techniques as well as traditional lore for exploring the Celtic
Otherworld.
Paperback: 978-1-78099-615-8 ebook: 978-1-78099-616-5

Traditional Witchcraft for the Woods and Forests
A Witch's Guide to the Woodland with Guided Meditations and
Pathworking
Melusine Draco
A Witch's guide to walking alone in the woods, with guided
meditations and pathworking.
Paperback: 978-1-84694-803-9 ebook: 978-1-84694-804-6

Wild Earth, Wild Soul
A Manual for an Ecstatic Culture
Bill Pfeiffer
Imagine a nature-based culture so alive and so connected,
spreading like wildfire. This book is the first flame...
Paperback: 978-1-78099-187-0 ebook: 978-1-78099-188-7

Naming the Goddess
Trevor Greenfield
Naming the Goddess is written by over eighty adherents and
scholars of Goddess and Goddess Spirituality.
Paperback: 978-1-78279-476-9 ebook: 978-1-78279-475-2

Shapeshifting into Higher Consciousness
Heal and Transform Yourself and Our World with Ancient
Shamanic and Modern Methods
Llyn Roberts
Ancient and modern methods that you can use every day
to transform yourself and make a positive difference in the
world.
Paperback: 978-1-84694-843-5 ebook: 978-1-84694-844-2

Readers of ebooks can buy or view any of these
bestsellers by clicking on the live link in the title. Most
titles are published in paperback and as an ebook.
Paperbacks are available in traditional bookshops. Both
print and ebook formats are available online.

Find more titles and sign up to our readers' newsletter at
http://www.johnhuntpublishing.com/paganism
Follow us on Facebook at
https://www.facebook.com/MoonBooks
and Twitter at https://twitter.com/MoonBooksJHP